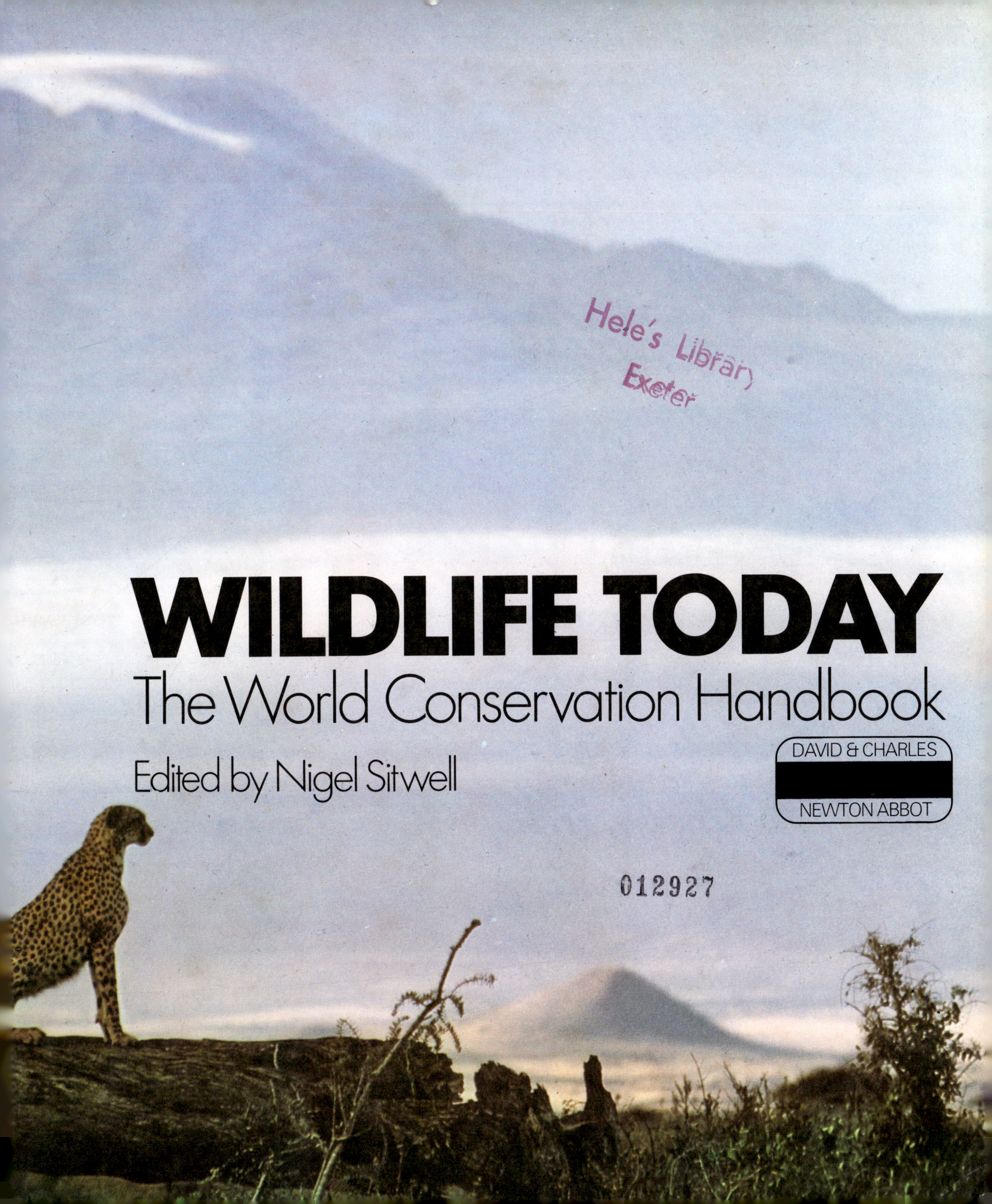

WILDLIFE TODAY

The World Conservation Handbook

Edited by Nigel Sitwell

DAVID & CHARLES
NEWTON ABBOT

STAFF CREDITS
Editor: Nigel Sitwell
Picture Director: Alexander Low
Art Director: Tom Deas
Design: Richard Kelly
      Venetia Greville Bell
Project Co-ordinator: Emma Stacey
Cartography: Ron Hayward

ISBN 0 7153 6780 3

Copyright © David & Charles Limited

Printed in Italy by Librex, Milan

Contributors

Contents

Foreword *by HRH The Duke of Edinburgh* — 6

Introduction *by Roger Tory Peterson* — 8

Wildlife Men of Today — 10

Section 1 · LARGE MAMMALS
Can the Tiger Survive? *by Guy Mountfort* — 12
Spotted Cats & the Fur Trade *by Norman Myers* — 18
Orang-Utan *by Tom Harrisson* — 24
The Polar Bear—A Brighter Future *by Dr David Stonegate* — 28
The Giant Panda *by Janet Barber* — 34

Section 2 · SMALLER MAMMALS
The Threatened Lemurs *by Dr Robert Martin* — 38
The Bawean Deer Breeds *by Nigel Sitwell* — 46
The Vicuna Recovers *by Dr Hartmut Jungius* — 50

Section 3 · BIRDS
The Peregrine Falcon
The Peregrine in Britain *by Dr Derek A. Ratcliffe* — 56
The Peregrine in N. America *by Richard W. Fyfe* — 59
West Indian Parrots *by Dr Cameron B. Kepler* — 62
The Birds of the Seychelles *by Malcolm Penny* — 68
New Laws for Italian Birds *by Arturo Osio* — 74

Section 4 · MARINE ENVIRONMENT
The Great Whales *by Nigel Sitwell* — 76
Commercial Sealing *by Colin Platt* — 84
The Sea Otter Success Story *by Nicole Duplaix-Hall* — 90

Section 5 · REPTILES AND AMPHIBIANS
Poachers Still Hunt the Alligator *by George Laycock* — 94
Giant Tortoises
Giant Tortoises on Aldabra *by Tony Beamish* — 100
Giant Tortoises on the Galápagos *by Dr Roger Perry* — 103

Section 6 · INSECTS AND PLANTS
The Butterfly Trade *by John A. Burton* — 108
Protecting the Redwoods *by John V. Smith* — 112
Endangered Plants *by Jon Tinker* — 116

Section 7 · SAVING THE HABITATS
Introduction — 120
The Camargue *by Christopher W. Savage* — 122
Lake Nakuru *by Drs M. F. I. J. Bijleveld* — 126
Yellowstone's Centenary *by Robert Sanders* — 128

Emergency Action Summary — 130

The World Wildlife Fund — 138

Index — 141

The prevailing hysteria about the environment has tended to obscure the whole purpose of conservation. It is, of course, true that the increasing human population, together with the exploitation of natural resources, the growth of industries and the spread of pollution, are all at the root of the conservation problem, but that is only part of the picture. The International Union for Conservation of Nature and Natural Resources, the World Wildlife Fund and many other national and international organisations are deeply involved in the more practical business of trying to prevent the extinction of wild populations of animals and plants.

It will not be much use if, after spending so much time and effort on cleaning up the whole environment and limiting the population, we wake up to find that, in the meantime, whole lists of creatures and plants have disappeared from the face of the earth. The general problem of the discharge of oil at sea is obviously serious, but the killing of the last remaining whales is a disaster. The general problem of industrial pollution is serious, but the real disaster is when it destroys the ecology and unique life forms in specific lakes and rivers. The vast problem of world population growth is not going to be solved overnight, but the gradual erosion, by human infiltration, of the few national parks and reserves, which already exist or which could be created now, is a far more immediate and desperate difficulty.

It is these immediate issues which will be considered by this publication. There is bound to be a lot of bad news, but I hope there will be enough good news, thanks to the efforts of the I.U.C.N., the W.W.F. and others, to give all supporters of the cause of conservation grounds for encouragement and hope.

7

Introduction

Naturalists and biologists have been sounding the warning of world-wide ecological disaster for at least a generation. Books such as Paul Sears' *Deserts on the March*, William Vogt's *Road to Survival*, and Fairfield Osborne's *Our Plundered Planet* were passionate pleas for a long critical look at what we are doing to the natural world. These books, written by scholarly men who not only had done their homework, but who were also articulate, met with mixed reactions; their authors were plainly prophets ahead of their time.

Perhaps Rachel Carson's *Silent Spring* did more than any other publication to bring about the breakthrough of ecological awareness on the part of the general public that took place in the decade between 1960 and 1970, and which culminated in the Stockholm Conference of 1972. Rachel Carson's main target was DDT, which we now recognize as only one of a large family of pesticides with residual properties inimical to wildlife. And pesticides are but one aspect of the widespread pollution that affects not only wildlife, but inevitably man himself.

But why has the naturalist and especially the bird-watcher so often performed the role of prophet? To put it simply, birds and other animals are sensitive indicators of the environment that send out signals when things slip out of balance. Birds in particular, because of their high rate of metabolism and furious pace of living, act as a sort of environmental litmus-paper. They are far more than nuthatches and finches to be fed at the window shelf, robins to enliven the garden, waterfowl to be shot, or rare waders to be ticked off on the bird-watcher's checklist. As an obsessed bird-watcher who could not endure a silent, birdless spring, I am aware that a world in which birds could no longer exist would also be a world in which man could probably not survive.

In this book we are concerned mostly with endangered species. A glance at the table of contents will reveal that the majority of forms treated might be termed 'glamor species'; we are presented with a skimming of the surface cream of endangered wildlife. Parrots and peregrines are glamorous, little brown birds are not. Polar bears excite the popular imagination, small rodents or lesser marsupials, no matter how rare, seldom do. Asian butterflies are discussed by John Burton, but pause a moment to consider how many beetles and other less flamboyant insects must be in similar trouble because of pesticides, pollution, and environmental attrition.

The larger and more spectacular species have always been the first to succumb to direct persecution by man, and contrary to popular myth it was not solely modern man in recent times who was the agent of extinction. As the late James Fisher so persuasively argued, Stone-Age man was almost certainly responsible for the disappearance of a great many of the larger animals, the 'megafauna', whenever his hordes invaded a new continental area. Island faunas were even more vulnerable.

Although extinction is to some extent a natural process, with far more species lost in millenia past than exist on earth today, an equilibrium of sorts is maintained by the slow evolutionary rise of new species, the product of adaptive radiation. During the last four centuries, however, concurrent with man's explosive population growth and technological development, we have lost species at a much accelerated rate. Using the evidence of the fossil record and his slide-rule, James Fisher estimated that in recent decades we have been losing species at three or four times the rate of natural extinction (my own 'guesstimate' is at least twelve times). In the scholarly book *Wildlife Crisis*, co-authored with Prince Philip, Fisher pointed out that the greatest number of bird and mammal species were lost during the two decades around the turn of the century, roughly from 1890 to 1910. This was a low point in the fortunes of wildlife and a turning point in the public conscience. Management practices and legal restrictions in many countries soon brought hunting into line with the philosophy that only the removable surplus should be cropped. Many persecuted non-game species were given protection; sanctuaries and preserves proliferated. During the decades between 1910 and 1960 there was a steady diminution in the number of additional species that were lost. Direct persecution and killing (except for the disastrous commercial exploitation of whales) was no longer the principal vehicle of decimation. The late 1950s and the 1960s, however, saw wildlife conservation facing a new crisis for much more subtle environmental reasons, inexorably linked with human over-population pressures.

Chlorinated hydrocarbons and other residual poisons, already detected at the ends of the earth, now threaten many birds that are at the ends of long food chains, especially fish-eating birds and bird-eating birds. The eastern North American population of the peregrine is now completely gone between Georgia and Hudson's Bay. Locally, the osprey, bald eagle, and brown pelican are laying thin-shelled eggs and reproduction is dangerously low. These are only some of the more publicized species in trouble. The widespread disappearance of many butterflies and moths (especially the attractive large Saturnids) is almost certainly linked to pollutants.

Second only to pollution, attrition of the environment has become the greatest threat, particularly in the rapidly developing tropical countries. In fact, we are almost certain to lose many species of the humid climax forests in tropical America and in South-East Asia in the very near future, if indeed some of them have not already gone. We will not find many of these on the endangered list of the International Union for Conservation of Nature, for there is no way to assess their thinly distributed numbers on a continental basis. No one knows their real status. Quite the opposite of species inhabiting tropical islands such as the Seychelles, which are limited in area and can be censused fairly easily.

I predict that we will soon lose more species in the American tropics, particularly in the fast disappearing forests of the northern Andes, than in any other part of the world. And most of them will go with no one taking note of their passing.

Wildlife Men of Today

*Guy Coheleach **(right)** with US Vice President, Spiro Agnew.*

Guy Coheleach

by Roger A. Caras

Snowy egrets, by Guy Coheleach

If you like to have neat categories into which to fit people you will have trouble handling wildlife artist Guy Coheleach. He has been described as a 'halfback who paints' and as a 'painter who plays halfback'. He has been labeled the 'fastest brush in the East' because of his legendary frontal assault on any bare canvas that comes his way. One observer noted that a bare canvas was not only a challenge to Guy Coheleach but an affront. 'He has so much to say it is almost as if a new canvas represents failure until he can get at it, fill it, and turn it into success.'

In fact, it is energy that characterizes Guy Coheleach and everything he does. When told he was wasting time as a commercial artist, Guy promptly abandoned a highly lucrative career and switched to what he really cared about all along—natural history. He never looked back: within five years of starting his first wildlife portrait he had a commission from the US Department of State. He was to paint a bald eagle for the Vice-President to present as a gift from the American people to a foreign head of state.

Without doubt it is this energy that distinguishes the Coheleach canvas from all others. Guy, with sureness of the animal he portrays, senses *their* energy. And it is energy as well as beauty that he records. In a falcon stooping to the kill, in the marauding owl at dusk, the sense of energy is relatively easy to convey. But, even in repose, the tigers, leopards, elephants, hawks, and lesser birds of Guy Coheleach are packed with the power of life. Inevitably the beholder feels the fierce energy that keeps them alive in a world where lesser creatures must perforce fail that test. All of that is relentlessly present in every Coheleach canvas. It is the theme of his work. It represents his awe. It tells a great deal about his capacity for reverence.

One of nine children of Gaetan Guy and Flavia Marie Aymong Coheleach, Guy has the perfectionist's drive true to his French–Swiss background. Brought up in Baldwin, Long Island, he commuted each morning to Brooklyn to attend Bishop Loughlin Parochial High School to which he had won a scholarship, to New York's famed Cooper Union where he learned his first but soon-to-be-abandoned trade as a commercial artist. There was a tour with the Army in Engineer-Intelligence, and duty in both Korea and Vietnam.

Perhaps it is the desire for perfection that drives him, something that has haunted Guy for as long as he can remember. Or possibly it is the knowledge that time is running out on him. For Guy Coheleach is well aware of the fact that he will be one of the last wildlife artists on earth to have living models. He quietly dreads the rapid disappearance of the beauty and truth that he finds reflected in wild creatures. His frequent trips afield, in North America, in Africa, and recently in Asia, have given him a yardstick. He can and has gauged emotionally as well as intellectually the thinning out that is occurring. When he speaks of these matters his temper flares but he soon becomes quiet and withdraws into his sadness.

The accomplishments of Guy Coheleach are recorded well on the library shelves, in the books that contain his art and on the walls of the discerning. His name (which almost everybody pronounces incorrectly—it is KOH-LEE-ACK) is known to millions of people, and he is in demand for lectures and television appearances. But if he is successful by contemporary standards, he nevertheless cannot forget the source of his success, the wildlife he paints. And so he helps conservation by donating original paintings and prints. In the past five years Guy Coheleach's paintings have helped raise over $2 million (£800,000) for various conservation groups.

Guy Coheleach's paintings are beautiful: so say the museums that now buy and covet them, the thousands of owners of reproductions that already sell for hundreds of dollars, and the top magazines who bid for his services. But Guy remembers the beauty of his subjects, the source of his inspiration. It is why he donates his paintings to raise money for their conservation.

David Shepherd

by Nigel Sitwell

David Shepherd's one ambition at the age of eighteen was to be a game warden—and he traveled all the way from Britain to Nairobi, Kenya, to apply for a job. He makes an amusing story out of this episode now, remarking wryly that 'the job lasted as long as it took Mervyn Cowie (then Director of the Kenya National Parks) to say no'. It was not until a decade later that David again linked up with his childhood ambition, via the medium of his paintbrush.

Back in England, David Shepherd deliberated between 'earning a living as a bus driver' and 'starving as an artist'. He chose to starve. Taken under the wing of the marine and portrait painter Robin Goodwin, after failing the entrance examination for London's prestigious Slade School of Art, he eventually became a professional artist, specializing for his first ten years in aviation and military subjects. But then in 1960, while in Kenya as a guest of the Royal Air Force, David 'accidentally started painting jumbos'. (He usually calls them 'jumbos'— seldom 'elephants'—and is inclined to prefer 'animals' to 'zoology'.) From this point on, he concentrated on painting wildlife, in particular the wildlife of Africa, and above all, elephants.

Though justly famed for his animal paintings, David Shepherd still paints other subjects. Aircraft, for instance, and magnificent steam locomotives (another Shepherd passion: he owns two of them himself, weighing in at 313,600 pounds (140 English tons) apiece and bought from British Railways who were about to scrap them). He also paints portraits, and his subjects have included Britain's Queen Mother, the Ruler of Abu Dhabi, and Zambian President Kenneth Kaunda. How can one

artist excel in such seemingly different fields? David's answer is that they are not different—'they are all landscapes'—reasoning that an African landscape naturally has elephants and rhinos in it, as naturally as a railroad station has locomotives in it.

It is wildlife, however, that David Shepherd paints most, and cares about with a consuming passion. And his feeling is shown by the fact that over the years he has contributed very substantially to conservation work by donating his paintings for auction, or allowing them to be used on greeting cards. 'Animals have given me so much—happiness, success, financial freedom—that I want to give them something back.'

His biggest gift so far to the animal kingdom is a Bell Jet Ranger helicopter. To be strictly accurate, it was given to the Zambia Game Department, for anti-poaching duties, in late 1971. David organized the whole project. Enlisting the aid of other British artists, he raised some $115,000 (about £46,000) through the sale of paintings; his own work accounted for three-quarters of the sum raised. As I walked with him through the 16-acre garden of his Elizabethan farmhouse near the village of Godalming, not far from London, he told me gleefully that 'his' helicopter had already caught more than 500 poachers. Piloted by a young American with several thousand hours' experience in Jet Rangers (including combat experience in Vietnam), the helicopter is having a significant effect on Zambia's poaching problem. And its effect is indirect, too, for the word has got around, and now poachers run for cover at the sight of *any* helicopter —whether or not it is the anti-poaching patrol.

When I interviewed David three years ago he said that his favorite animal after the elephant was the tiger. It was, therefore, no surprise to learn that he was not long back from a trip to India—at his own expense—to gather the material for some tiger paintings. These are to be his own contribution to the World Wildlife Fund's Operation Tiger, and, like his other donated paintings, one will be auctioned—probably in the United States. He will paint a second tiger, which he plans to give to Mrs Gandhi for auctioning in India for the same cause.

As I left he was putting the finishing touches to a painting of lions in the Serengeti, commissioned by golfer Jack Nicklaus, and preparing to start work on his tiger paintings. I asked him why he gave so much of his effort to conservation. He told me, half in jest, that he is a compulsive painter and already pays tax at a high rate: 'I'd rather see this money put to work to help wildlife than vanish into the taxman's pocket'. But the real reason comes through very strongly when you are with David Shepherd. He is a man who not only gives intense pleasure to the many who own his original paintings and reproduction prints but also one who is making a major contribution to conserving the world's wild animals which he cares about so deeply. David Shepherd likes wild animals—and safeguarding their survival is perhaps even more important to him than painting them.

'Tsavo Waterhole', by David Shepherd

11

Can the Tiger Survive?

Spotted Cats & the Fur Trade

The Orang-utan

The Polar Bear – A Brighter Future

The Giant Panda

Guy Mountfort

Can the Tiger Survive?

Probably the most exciting news that tiger enthusiasts have had in recent years came in July 1972 from Indonesia. First came a report that Forestry Department officials in Bali had seen a tiger. The significance of this can be understood when it is realized that although common in 1914, the Bali tiger had become rare by 1920, and the last one had supposedly been shot by 1937. So for a tiger to suddenly turn up out of the blue, after having been presumed extinct for thirty years, is a startling event. Of course, many will be sceptical about the report, but let us hope that it is true and that there is still a small colony surviving.

The other good news from Indonesia concerned the Javan tiger. The population was reported at ten by the Forestry Department—and apparently two young had been seen. Though not thought to be extinct, the Javan race was considered on its last legs: once plentiful, it had declined throughout this century to an estimated five animals—until the latest report. Though the local human population regards tigers as the reincarnation of the souls of their departed kinsmen, the animals do not seem to have been held in particular reverence and allowed to go unmolested. On the contrary, they were everywhere enthusiastically hunted. Even if the latest news is confirmed, the Javan tiger cannot be regarded as safe with such a tiny population.

The Bali and the Javan tigers are two of the eight races of the tiger living in Asia. Though the most seriously threatened, they are not alone in their plight. All races of the tiger are listed in the *Red Data Book* of the International Union for Conservation of Nature. They are endangered—this much is known—but reliable and detailed information is very difficult to obtain. Animals which inhabit open country present little difficulty; and one can count creatures like caribou by aerial photography. But the tiger is self-effacing and lives in terrain

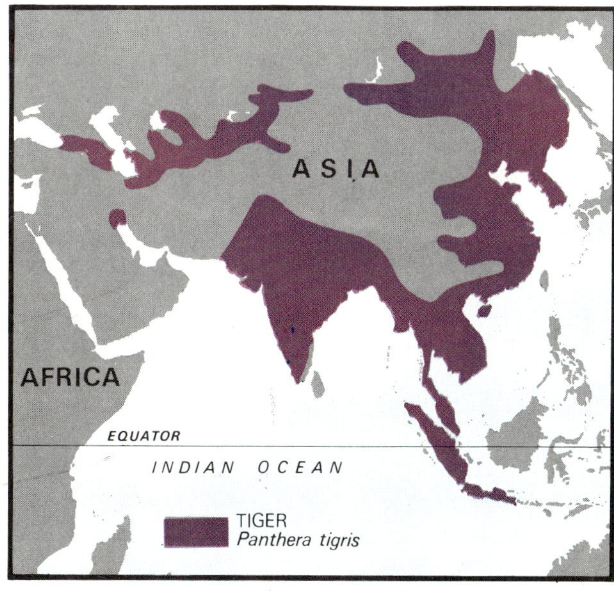

A tiger 'shikar' in the days of the British raj.
The Maharajah of Bikaner and a few of his trophies.

Population of the Tiger

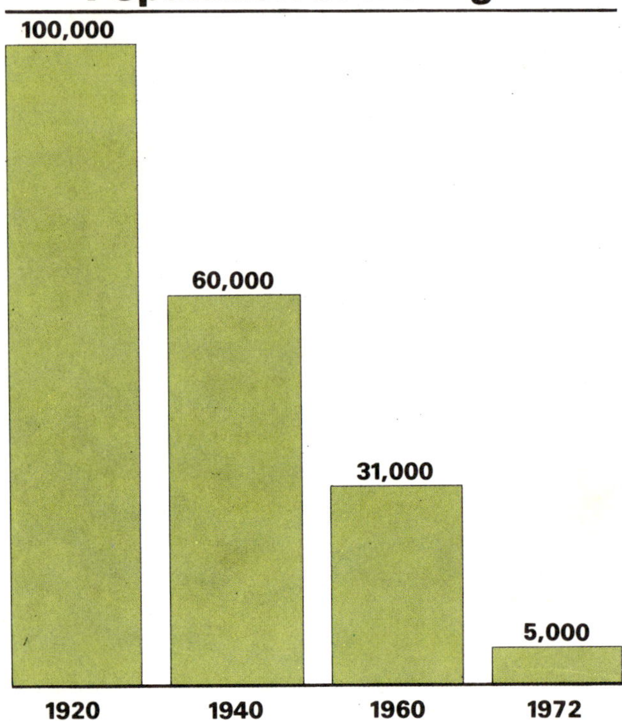

which provides ample cover and difficult access. Here is a brief run-down of the current status of the various races.

The Siberian tiger is a tremendously powerful animal which today survives only in a few isolated regions of the Amur valley and in the Sikhote-Alin mountains in the Soviet Far East. There may also be a few scattered through north-east China and Korea. However, the total remaining numbers of this race—not much more than 130—may be too small to maintain a viable breeding population.

The neighboring Chinese race is very little known. But what we do know is that, according to the *Red Data Book*, 'official Chinese policy encourages its destruction, as it is regarded as a menace to human life and a hindrance to agricultural and pastoral progress'. It is surely headed for extinction.

The Indo-Chinese race presents a relatively more cheerful picture. But only relatively, for everywhere it is known to be declining steeply. It is very unlikely that anything approaching the 1954 estimate of 3,000 is still accurate. Ranging over a huge area of Vietnam, Laos, Cambodia, eastern Burma, Thailand, and the Malay Peninsula to Singapore, It has suffered heavy losses from the holocaust of warfare that has swept back and forth across that troubled region. War is hell for wildlife as well as humans. And where there has been no war, there has been forest exploitation, land clearance, road-building, hunting, and the skin trade to contend with. This race of the tiger could well outlive the others but it is hard to believe it can escape extinction beyond the end of the present century, unless given protection.

In the large island of Sumatra, the tiger was not considered in need of protection in 1936, but by 1965 its status had seriously deteriorated. Today it survives only in the northern part of the island and in the mountainous region of the south-west. No good estimate of its numbers exists, but it is certainly now in the very low hundreds. The destruction of its natural prey and the constant erosion of its habitat by the growing human population cause the tigers to prey increasingly on domestic livestock. Consequently they are vigorously hunted, not only with guns but by means of baited cage-traps and pit-falls armed with bamboo spears.

The prospect for the Caspian tiger is equally depressing. Once found in the Soviet Union, Iran, and Afghanistan, it was exterminated in the Soviet Union by 1950, and the last evidence of its presence in Afghanistan was a set of pug-marks on the banks of the river Oxus in 1965. Only in Iran might it still survive; about fifteen are thought to remain in the Elburz mountains.

Finally, we come to the best known or Indian race, the so-called 'Royal' Bengal tiger. It has been the favorite trophy of kings, princes, maharajahs, and sportsmen for many centuries. There was competition between the Indian princes to out-do each other in organizing bigger and bigger tiger hunts, or *shikars*, and the bags were enormous. One maharajah claimed in 1965, to have shot

The tiger's normal prey varies considerably according to locality and opportunity, but includes deer, wild pigs, and buffaloes—even creatures as small as lizards and frogs. Nowadays tigers also prey on domestic cattle—for which they are widely persecuted.

1,150 tigers during his lifetime. During the period of the British raj, tiger hunting was the pastime of nearly all army officers and government officials. Everyone behaved as though the supply was inexhaustible.

The Indian tiger used to occupy virtually the whole of India, Nepal, Sikkim, Bhutan, Bangladesh, and western Burma (and the Indus valley of Pakistan until 1886). The present range remains much the same, but the population has shrunk to a tiny fraction of its former size and is now fragmented into small groups scattered over an area as large as Europe. In 1930 it was estimated that there were still 40,000 tigers in the Indian sub-continent. In 1939 the figure was revised to 30,000. By 1970 the figure for India was put at 1,500, with perhaps 200 each in Nepal and Bhutan, and another 100 in what is now Bangladesh. Sikkim still has a few, and so probably has western Burma.

It is abundantly clear that time is not on the side of the tiger. Where tigers are thinly scattered into small isolated groups they will almost certainly die out. In the case of the Javan and Caspian races, the best solution would probably be to bring the few surviving animals into captivity. This may have to be considered for the Sumatran and Siberian races, too, before long. In time the zoos might even be able to return a population of the offspring to the wild.

The only hope for the remaining tigers in the wild is to concentrate on the Indian and perhaps the Indo-

Laotian villagers returning from a successful hunt. The meat is eaten, but is liked more for the strength it is supposed to give than its flavor.

A tiger skin stretched out to dry, also in Laos. A starving dog later ate away one foot.

CURRENT STATUS OF THE TIGER

Race	Present estimate	Survival prospects
Bali tiger *P.t. balica*	Possible remnant population	Extinction inevitable
Siberian tiger *P.t. altaica*	USSR perhaps 130; N-E China and Korea, a few	Extinction probable
Chinese tiger *P.t. amoyensis*	Scattered remnants constantly persecuted	Extinction probable
Indo-Chinese tiger *P.t. corbetti*	Perhaps 2,000 scattered over huge area and widely persecuted	May survive a few decades, but eventual extinction probable
Sumatran tiger *P.t. sumatrae*	In low hundreds and persecuted	Extinction probable within 25 years
Javan tiger *P.t. sondaica*	About 10 left	Extinction inevitable
Caspian tiger *P.t. virgata*	Perhaps 15, in Iran only	Extinction probable
Indian tiger *P.t. tigris*	India—2,000? Bangladesh—100? Nepal—200? Bhutan—200? Sikkim and Burma, a few	Might be saved by strenuous effort. Otherwise extinction within 30–40 years

An Italian tourist was caught trying to smuggle these tiger and other skins out of India at Calcutta airport.

Chinese races, which have some protection and willing governments within their ranges; then to try to create a number of large and totally protected reserves with the right habitat and prey species. At least one each is needed for Bangladesh and Bhutan, and two or three each in India and Nepal; in each case these might be created by enlarging and improving existing reserves. India is already planning eight big tiger reserves. The Taman Negara National Park in Malaysia appears to offer the best chance for the Indo-Chinese tiger. The aim should be to establish an ultimate population of at least 100 tigers in each of these.

At the same time, of course, continued efforts must be made to stop the demand for tiger skin products in the developed nations. The United States has already banned the import of tiger skins, along with the skins of a variety of other endangered animals. Britain, too, has banned the import of tiger skins (though, regrettably, Britain does not forbid the import of made-up coats). Even the famed Guardsmen—familiar to tourists who watch the changing of the guard at London's Buckingham Palace —are playing their part, for even before the ban, the British armed services had agreed to buy no more leopard or tiger skins for their bandsmen's aprons. But still the poaching goes on, and the next move must be to close down the back-street black markets in India and its neighbors. Thousands of skins are held by small shopkeepers and they are also sold openly in the big hotels. The task is formidable, for undeclared skins are easily concealed, and there is no doubt that many are still being illegally smuggled by tourists, seamen, and airline staff.

Like the rock temples of Abu Simbel, which were saved at the last minute only by large-scale international effort and finance, the tiger *can* be saved. It will be a difficult and costly task, but not impossible. Those Asian countries I have mentioned, which are already wrestling with the almost insurmountable task of providing for 700 million needy people, cannot save the tiger on their own, however; they need, and deserve, the help of the rest of the world. The World Wildlife Fund is launching 'Operation Tiger'—a global appeal for $1 million in order to help create the special tiger reserves which are so urgently needed. It will be the biggest single effort yet made to save an endangered animal from extinction.

Norman Myers

Spotted Cats & the Fur Trade

Probably the best known and best loved of all wild animals are the large cats—and yet, as a group, they are probably under the most pressure from man. Early in 1971 a report was presented to an international meeting on the spotted cats calling for much tougher legislation in the consumer countries of North America and Western Europe. Dealing especially with jaguar and ocelot in the Amazon region, and leopard and cheetah in Africa, the report urged that greater protection be given to all the spotted cats, especially until more detailed investigations could be carried out to discover their true status.

Indications from many countries suggested that the spotted cats were being exterminated on a broad front, largely due to the demands of the international fur trade. How far individual species were actually in danger—or in danger of danger—was not so clear, but it was obvious that after a decade of talk it was now time to do something to establish their real position in their natural habitats across Latin America, Africa, and Asia. Were they declining everywhere? Were they declining faster than other creatures in the face of 'the normal process of development' in these emergent regions? (It is believed that in Kenya, for instance, the number of elephants killed each year to protect crops is increasing by 3 to 4 per cent—about the same rate of increase as the human population in that country.) Above all, was their decline largely the fault of the fur trade, or was it due to habitat disruption or because their prey animals were being eliminated?

Much has happened since early 1971. The United States has banned the import of spotted cat skins, and of live animals too. A number of countries in Europe have passed or are preparing legislation to impose similar bans. But as the usual markets dry up, the producers on the ground in Africa, Asia, and Latin America are shifting their attentions to Japan, where the consumer now wants to out-consume his neighbor, where the whole passion for spotted furs may follow the trend of the 1960s elsewhere, regardless of conservationists' warnings. Japan's record on whales is a gloomy portent. Japanese Joneses seem to prove no more capable of thinking for themselves than in other lands.

Moreover, a number of countries in Europe may ban only the actual skins of spotted cats. There will be no questions asked if a ready-made fur coat arrives at the port of entry. Japan will be only too ready to jump into such markets. Britain has attempted what is no doubt called a 'practical compromise', restricting imports of spotted furs to those with properly documented authority from the country of origin. If a skin arrives with the official stamp of, say, Sudan, that's fine (supposing that Sudan, unlike Kenya and a number of other African countries, still allows the export of skins). This implies that Sudan, a country the size of Western Europe, much of it desert or swamp, is able to police its huge area to ensure no unofficial skins from Kenya, Ethiopia, or other neighboring countries pass through its official channels. Africa does not have much money for such policing activities, particularly when it features sixteen out of the twenty-five poorest nations in the world. And even if it were very affluent, one wonders how it could keep check on such enormous territories when the United States cannot eliminate poaching of alligators from the Everglades Park, a tiny tip of Florida. For Britain to suppose that African countries could keep tight control of the spotted furs leaving their ports, even if they wanted to, is to suppose Africa is more populated with angels than Britain! To be effective, legislation must place a total prohibition on all furs of any particular species, from whatever source—as a minimum measure.

In the meantime, the furriers themselves seem to favor stronger protection than the British Government. Their International Federation has recommended its members to institute a three-year moratorium on leopard and cheetah until the International Union for the Conservation of Nature can carry out a field investigation in Africa. The furriers have also recommended a ban on clouded leopards and snow leopard (as well as tiger, and other species). They do not agree, however, that there is need for a similar stay on trade in jaguar and ocelot on which the IUCN is conducting a survey in Latin America too. (Not that all furriers are observing the bans; officials will not say how many, whether half, or three-quarters, or one-tenth).

So much for action by the consumer countries. Without cooperation on both sides there is little prospect of progress. But the producer countries have long been ahead of their opposite numbers in trying to protect spotted cats from undue depletion. Brazil has now banned all trade in spotted furs, and so have various other countries of Latin America. But as long as one country won't play ball, such as Colombia, there is a loophole through which you can fly a freight plane—as has been the practice from Colombia's jungle outpost, Leticia, funnelling illicit furs from Brazil, Venezuala, and Peru. So much, again, for Britain's notion that people don't break the rules, even when a man in the rain forest can double his year's income with a sackful of hides.

Of more consequence in the long run, however, for jaguars and ocelots will be developments like the Trans-Amazon Highway. This road is to run 3,000 miles from the Atlantic westwards to the Andes. Its intention is not so much to send goods from one side of the continent to the other; it is to send landless people from Brazil's drought-stricken north-east into the middle of that lush forest region—there to stay. The worst disruption will not be so much the 600-yard gash cut by the road-builders, but the 50-mile swathe that will be slashed by the settlers as they pour into the new region and spread out as far as they can on either side; at least 200,000 square miles in the fairly near future alone. All this will mean many more people ready to set a trap for the jaguar in the next valley (or the valley thirty miles away), and

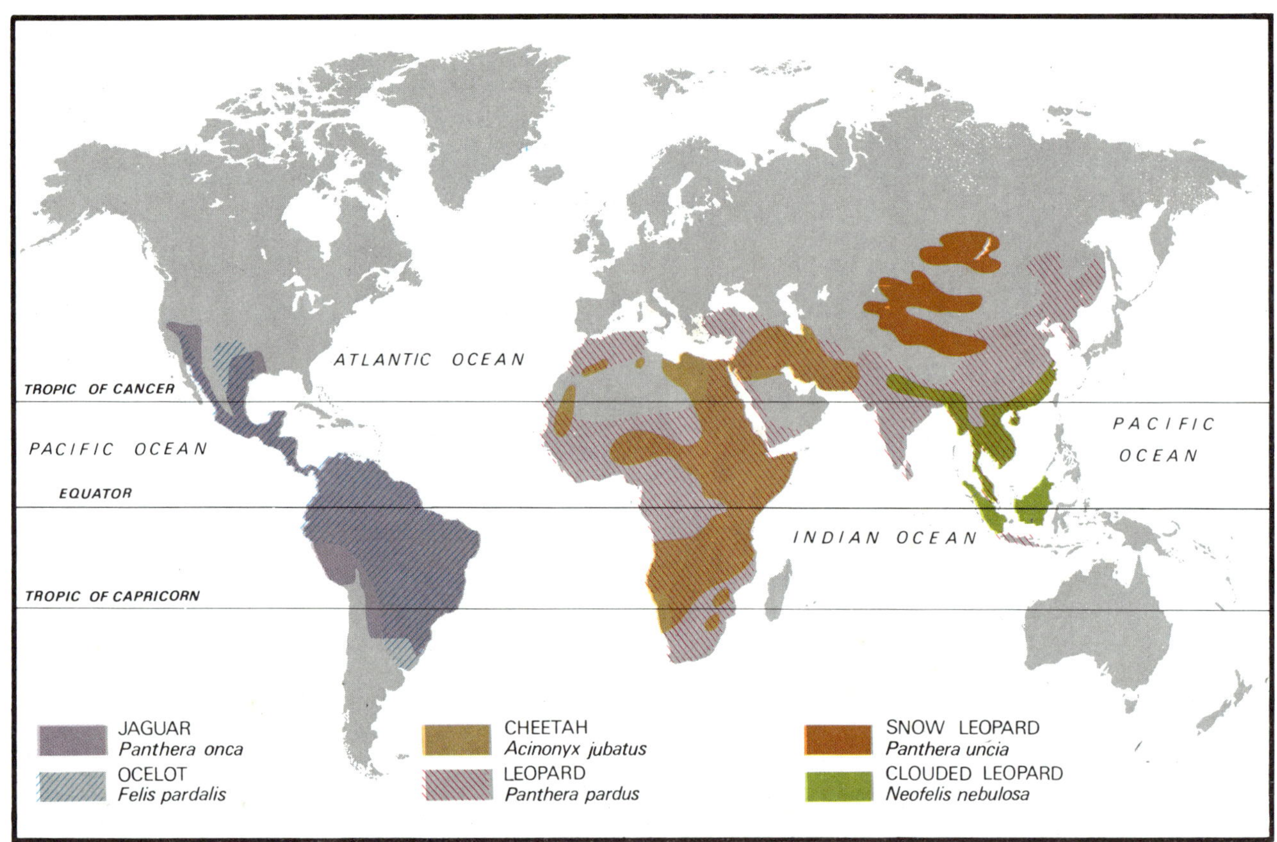

(Above) This African leopard, unique among the big cats, will carry its prey into a tree to devour it at leisure, safe from the attentions of scavengers. Despite poaching, leopards may prove to be the last of the large cats to survive in any number.

many more people ready to put every peccary and capybara into the pot. The full impact of the highway may not be apparent for several years. But there is no point waiting until the problem presents itself in plain terms. By then, it may well be too late.

In Asia, the plight of the tiger is a measure of how great cats are surviving in that overloaded environment. Some people on the spot believe the leopard may well be faring rather better, though still much worse than ten years ago. Very little is known about the clouded leopard, except that its position is probably precarious. The snow leopard is rather better documented, though still scantily. It is inclined to keep out of the forest zones, which means that in the eastern Himalaya region it is pretty much confined to the areas up towards the snow line. As one moves west, beyond Kashmir, the monsoon is far less effective, and so in Pakistan there are large gaps in the forest belt. This means a much deeper range for the clouded leopard, from 18,000 feet to as low as 7,000 feet. Some would say this means a better hope for survival through enlarged habitat; others would say it makes it all the more vulnerable to hunters from the lowlands.

In Africa, poaching has undoubtedly led to severe reduction of numbers in some areas. But the depredations of the illegal hunter may be nothing compared with the legitimate, indeed laudable, efforts of his six or eight off-spring in due course of time to provide for themselves. Africa is no longer the last great empty continent. In Kenya, for instance, the arable lands are already full beyond bursting-point, and people are spilling out into the savanna lands—the cheetah's main habitat. The countries of safari paradise, Uganda and Tanzania together with Kenya, already feature population growth-rates approaching 3.5 per cent, and may well become the first communities in the world to reach a 4 per cent growth rate by the end of the century, *i.e. doubling every seventeen years.* Kenya's savannalands will probably have to accommodate at least another twelve million people by the year 2000, more than the country's present total. The other countries of Africa will not be far behind in their swelling numbers; and if numbers are on the increase, so are expectations. While a peasant is being squeezed down to less than an acre, he will be all the more determined to grab two if he can find any to spare.

The cheetah in particular does not seem to like the idea of development. At first sign of ranch fencing, it is off, while a maize patch is less use to it than Times Square is to a herd of zebras. Even if the cheetah encounters little of the paraphernalia of modern ranching, as will probably be the case on Masai ranches for a good while yet, there is a threat from game cropping. Cropping could show local people what the wildlife is worth beyond the rather nebulous benefits of tourism. But what if cropping teams want to exploit the antelope populations to their sustainable limits, as they must if they are to show that they can produce the goods as well as cattle can; will there

20

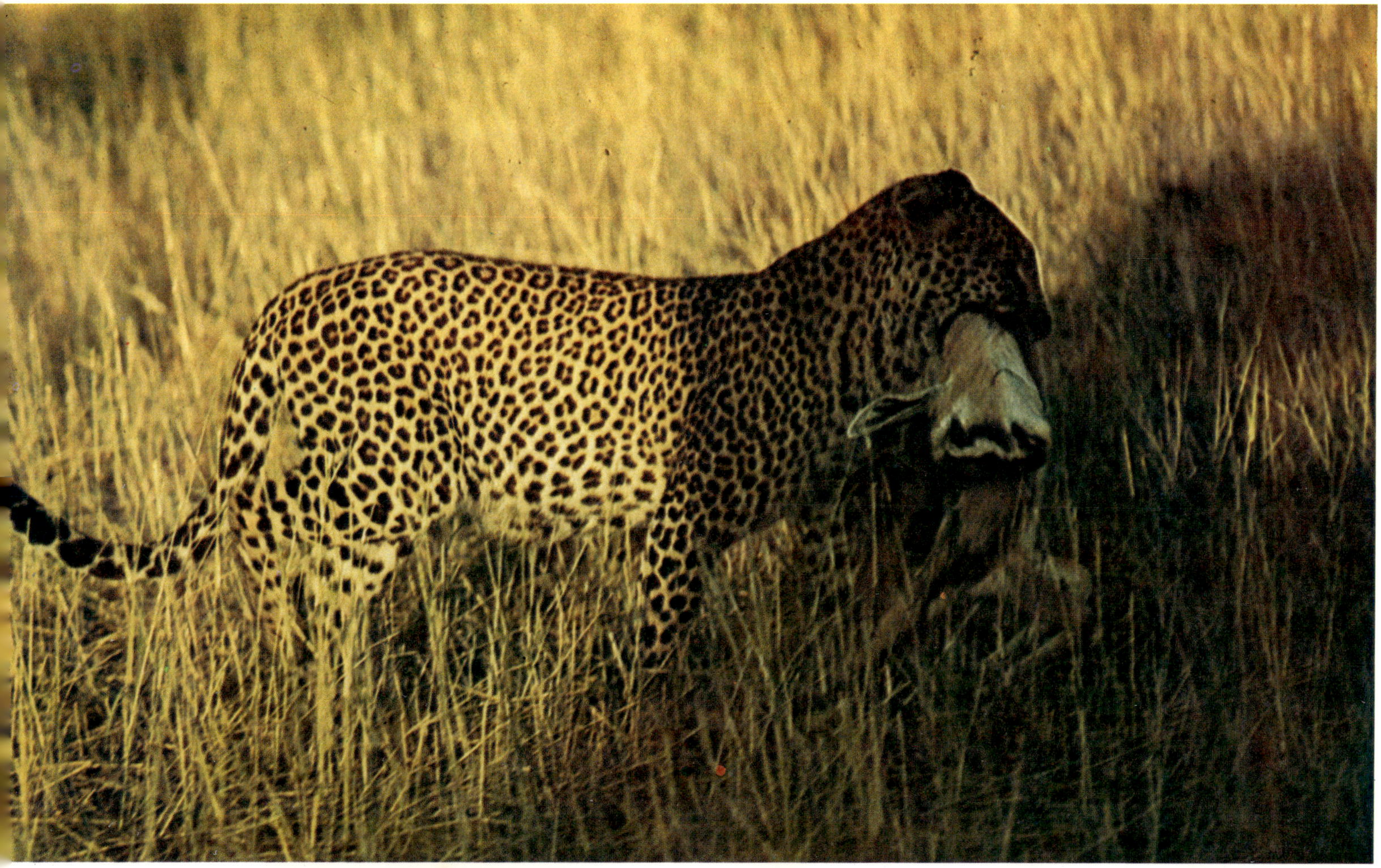

(Right) *The snow leopard lives between tree line (about 12,000 feet) and snow line (about 18,000 feet) in the great mountain ranges of Asia. With perhaps 500 left in the world, the snow leopard's chances of long-term survival are slim.*

then be any 'spare' antelopes or gazelles left for cheetah?

The leopard, by contrast, can live off the smell of an oil rag. Some experienced observers even suggest that the leopard could well be the last of Africa's great cats to be completely eliminated over large regions, that a few will still hold out somewhere long after the lion and cheetah

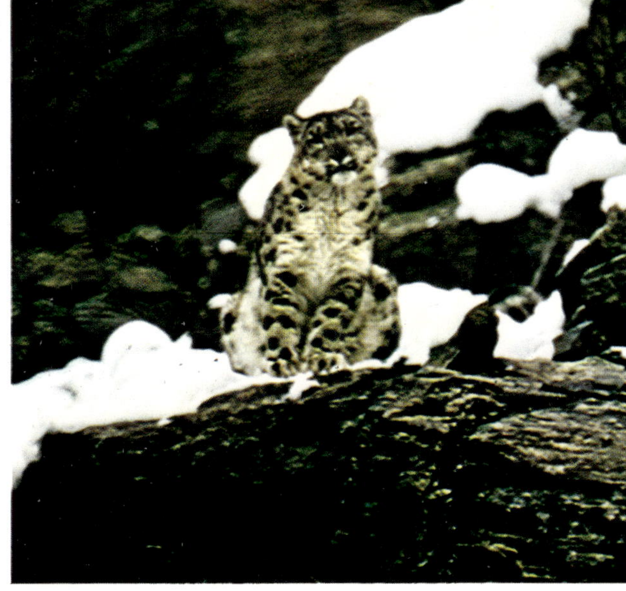

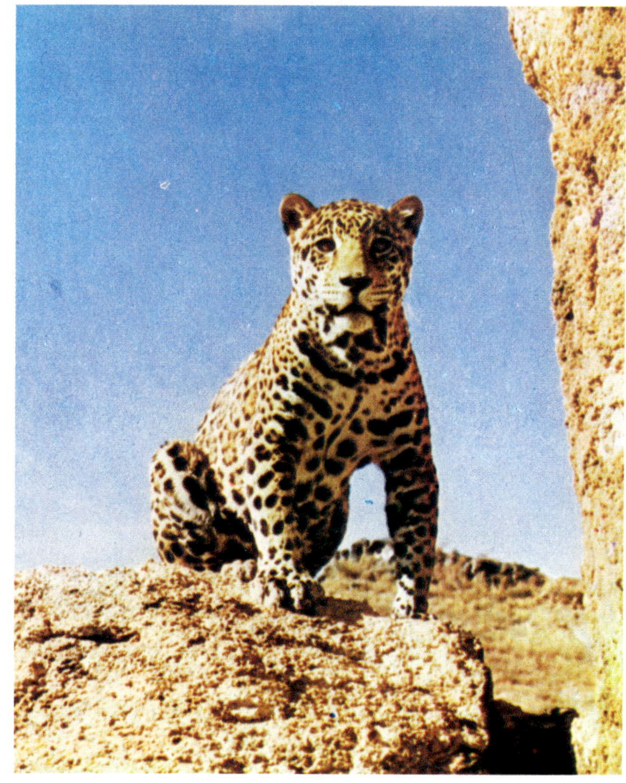

The jaguar is heavily poached throughout Latin America.

have disappeared from the scene. But is that what the world will settle for? Do we really think a few scattered individuals, which sense the penalties of revealing themselves to human eyes, are enough to constitute a species in full existence? How many is too few? Supposing leopard are grossly thinned out over much of Africa, but continue to live in fair numbers in that vast country, Botswana, where there are still only half a million people? Will that satisfy the consciences of those people who insist that African wildlife is not the affair of Africans alone?

A further threat may face cheetah in another huge, sparsely inhabited territory, adjacent to Botswana: South-West Africa. The urge to protect spotted cats in recent years has led to another fashion which may prove as harmful to the cheetah as the fur coat-trade has been. There is now a trend in places like Hollywood, Paris, and Hamburg to keep a pet cheetah around the house on the pretext of doing one's bit to protect an endangered creature from the poacher's cruel snare. Even more troublesome could be the notion that the way to save the cheetah is through special breeding centres in the developed countries. 'Safari parks' from California to Florida are justifying their huge numbers of cheetahs by suggesting that they are engaged in serious breeding programmes—though there is not a single such organization that has the necessary know-how, or can provide the right conditions. This is a cat that, unlike lions and leopards, rarely produces offspring in captivity. It is particularly unlikely to do so when as many as twenty-five are penned up in a single limited enclosure, typical of many a safari-land center.

Not that the conventional zoos are doing much better. Some famous establishments in the United States are reputed to be spending as much as a quarter of a million dollars on cheetah breeding programs. But there is a tendency to make sure the animals are available for the public to look at, rather than to provide them with the particular conditions, notably privacy, which they probably need to mate successfully.

What is needed is a concerted and serious attempt by all zoos to get together and try a co-operative breeding project, making sure that a lone female in one zoo is sooner or later permitted an extended encounter with a lone male from another zoo. The zoo officials might try to aim for what the cheetah thinks are the right conditions for breeding, not what humans hope will do. For instance, it has been suggested that breeding among cheetahs is dependent on a proper hormonal balance, which is in turn induced by plenty of space to run about in. A 'corridor' a few yards wide and a hundred yards long, which one prominent American zoo provides for its cheetahs, is absurdly inadequate. Some zoologists believe that the hormonal function is perhaps stimulated by hunting activity on the part of the cheetah. But when a few goats were occasionally let loose in the cheetah compound of one zoo, the public complained.

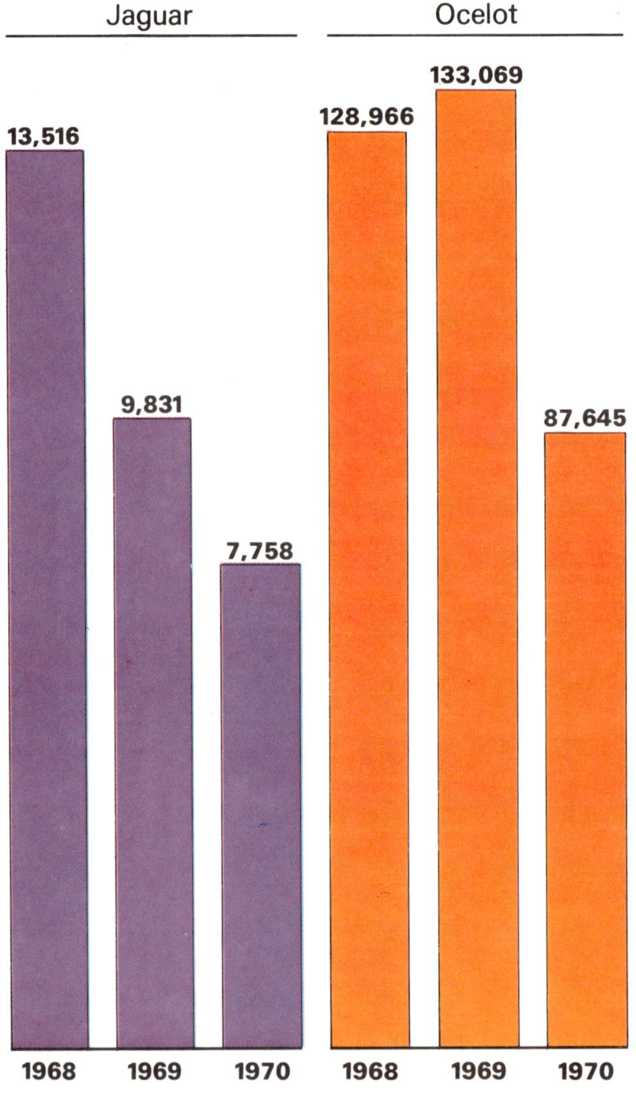

Some Asian countries, such as India, forbid trade in leopard and tiger skins, but others are not so strict: both are on display in the window of this souvenir shop in Bangkok, Thailand.

Fur skins imported into USA

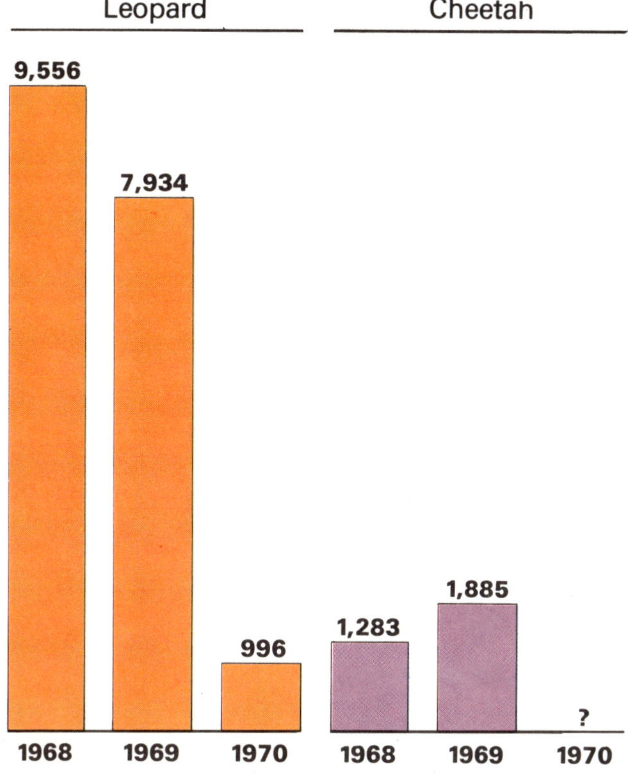

It is illegal to hunt jaguar in Brazil, or trade in their skins, but this did not deter the hunter above, who tracked his valuable prey for many days near the Surinam border, or those who continue to sell skins along the Amazon River **(below)**. The trade in spotted cat skins will go on as long as there is a demand. **(right)**

But if zoos can begin to breed animals like the cheetah, there would be less of a drain on the wild cheetah population. South-West Africa covers an enormous area, but cheetahs have never been very numerous there. And yet it is estimated that already something like 500 cheetahs have been taken from this one area alone for the world's zoos and safari-style establishments. If you add to this figure the number of animals which have died in the process, it is clear that South-West Africa is fast being denuded of its cheetahs. Interestingly, one of the men behind this trade is an internationally respected figure, renowned everywhere as one of the real fighters for Africa's wildlife!

Continuing with the cheetah as an example, though much the same could be said of the other spotted cats, it is clear that the public at large will have to make sacrifices if there are to be any wild cheetahs in Africa at all by the end of the century. Keeping patches of savanna available for the cheetah is going to be a costly business. Africans are not in much of a position to subsidize the world for the world's great natural heritage. Splendid though the donations channeled through the World Wildlife Fund, and other organizations, have been, the total is not a fraction of what will soon be required. If the people of Tanzania were to be compensated for what they will lose in upgraded ranching possibilities for the 12,000 square miles of the Serengeti ecosystem, they would need perhaps $20 million a year. This is over ten times what the

Serengeti earns through tourism at present. Moreover, the Serengeti only contains about 150 cheetahs. Coming low down in the carnivore clawing order, they probably cannot stand much competition from the 600 leopards, 2,000 lions, and 3,000 hyenas. To guard against disease and other natural disasters there would have to be several such areas set aside in Africa to ensure the cheetah a future.

The legislation against spotted cat products which has been introduced in the past year has certainly given new hope for a longer life for these exciting animals. But in the long run the answer to the problem will lie in politics and economics. It will depend on how much the advanced world is prepared to pay to help the emergent world solve its own pressing problems.

23

Tom Harrisson

Orang-utan

The scientific name of the orang-utan is *Pongo pygmaeus*, but it is a highly unsuitable one as the orang is neither a clown nor a pygmy. Big males far exceed the largest human being in size and strength (though they are normally the gentlest of creatures), and it is certainly one of the most beautiful, serious, and intelligent of the apes. The Malay name *orang-utan*, meaning 'man of the jungle', is much better.

The orang is the only fully arboreal great ape, and the present world population in the wild trees is estimated at between 5,000 and 10,000. Once numerous throughout South-East Asia and found abundantly in Stone Age cave food remains as far east as Celebes and north to China, this endlessly inquisitive, sensitive, alert animal has in historic times come to be confined to the two great islands of Borneo and Sumatra. Even within my eastern lifetime—I first went to central Borneo while still at college in 1932—orangs were fairly common in widely scattered areas of hill jungle (up to 5,000 feet), but mainly in lowland forest, on both islands.

Since the political and economic upheavals during and after the Second World War, these populations have been enormously reduced, so that of the four Borneo states, only Malaysian Sabah in the north and parts of Indonesian Kalimantan in the south-east still have viable, though dangerously fragmented, orang groupings. In Sumatra, recent fieldwork has shown that the remaining significant orang populations are in Atjeh and north-central Sumatra, only partly inside the theoretically conserved Gunung Loeser Reserve.

In 1971 transect counts and estimates for density gave up to three individual orangs per square kilometre in optimum sectors. (As the orang-utan seldom makes a loud sound, and is intensely mobile—the males very

24

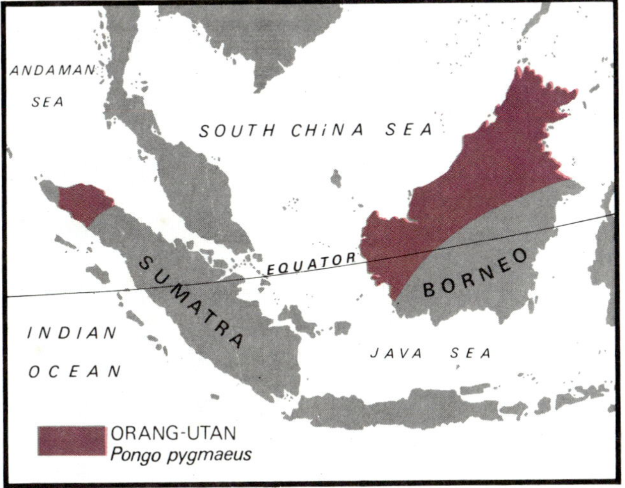

Rare photograph of wild orang-utans in north Sumatra, where the main threat is now destruction of the virgin forests which this arboreal ape needs to survive successfully.

often singly—statistical and other precise ecological information is hard to get.)

In the past year or so, a big new drive has been put in hand to salvage a once-more deteriorating situation. I say 'once more' because by the late 1960s, after two decades of effort, those of us deeply involved with the orang felt reasonably sure that the situation was under control, and the future for the species assured both in the wild and in captivity. This was a fair estimate at the time, based on the available evidence. But it is characteristic of the whole pattern of conservation that 'species security' does not *really* exist; above all, this applies in underdeveloped countries with massive economic (and educational) pressures and needs. So new crises threaten this and many other previously 'secured' life-forms in Indonesia, Malaysia, and elsewhere throughout the region.

To see how this new initiative has worked out, and what the next steps must be, we have to return to the causes of the catastrophic post-war decline in wild apes, which reached its peak in about 1955 and eased rapidly (temporarily?) after 1965.

In the 1950s the basic threat to the orang was demand from the world's zoos. No other animal was similarly threatened in South-East Asia—and there have been few similar cases of such intense pressure anywhere else in the world. Orangs are among the three or four most popular zoo exhibits in every continent. But they are particularly difficult to hunt down and capture. Jungle people and peasants have, in fact, carried out 99 per cent of the captures in the last quarter century. They have traded the animals down to the coasts, usually under appalling conditions of cruelty and inattention, with an enormous mortality rate. Moreover, the only way to catch an orang effectively, and economically, is to take a baby. Adults are too strong, adolescents too quick. The vast majority of the orangs that can be seen in zoos today were taken as babies from their mothers' arms— or, to be more exact, their mothers fell dead to the forest floor, and their babies were wrenched away. You kill the mother to get her child.

For every baby that reached a trader on the coast, at least another one died along the way. For these two babies, two fully grown, breathing females were deliberately slain as well. From the coast they were taken, usually in small boats, to the great trading *entrepôt* at Singapore, which became the center for orang traffic by air throughout the world. All this without legal or any other kind of control anywhere along the line.

This was one of the very few ways that the economically depressed island people could get any large sum of money at one time—especially the then beloved American dollars. A baby orang, safely delivered, could be worth enough money for a family to live on for years, though normally most of the profit went into the hands of middlemen and dealers.

At this stage, sustained and energetic action through the Survival Service Commission of the International Union for Conservation of Nature (IUCN) began to bear fruit. Indeed, an analysis of SSC minutes and agenda in the 1960s shows that the orang occupied more Commission attention, by frequency, than any other species in the world. Through adequate field evidence on this appalling traffic, we were able to prevail on the governments of the breeding areas to control it there, and on the government of Singapore to clamp down on the traffic. Hong Kong and other countries receiving overspill orangs presently came into line. It was a slow and painful business. It took so long for the message to get back to the hunters that the hunt was no longer worth the effort. And the message has not wholly got through yet! Wherever there is a desperate need for money and food, people may take an orang just on the chance that they can sell it.

The success of this campaign meant, however, that a lot of baby orangs were left stranded around the region. Partly to deal with this problem, Barbara Harrisson set up an organization called OURS (Orang-Utan Recovery Service), run in association with selected zoos, to collect, care for, and sponsor healthy babies and eventually place them in the best possible captive breeding environment. This operation was successful, and—which is exceptional in conservation—economically self-supporting.

At the same time we had our house at Kuching (the capital of Sarawak, Borneo), full of orangs in all sorts of stages of recovery, convalescence, and transit. It soon seemed ridiculous to send them all away to zoos, when there was a shortage even in the wilds of Borneo itself, on our doorstep. Thus the first wild re-training scheme was developed in the Bako National Park, about twenty miles down-river from Kuching in the Sarawak River Delta. Here, for the first time, retrieved orphan orangs which had been torn from their mothers' arms before they could climb, were taught the ways of the wild afresh, by Barbara Harrisson and a Sarawak Museum team.

Presently it seemed better to transfer the Bako scheme

500 miles to the north, to the less-populated sister-state of Sabah (North Borneo). There, under the able guidance of the Game Warden, G. S. de Silva, the wild-release scheme was further developed at Sepilok. It has now been running for nearly a decade. Two females have already bred in this semi-wild state, one of them certainly fertilized by a wild male. There are more than twenty orangs roaming free at Sepilok. The oldest is aged fifteen.

Orangs continued to be exported to zoos throughout the 1960s. But increasingly in a legal and orderly manner, with the organized approval of the Indonesian and Malaysian authorities, acting under SSC guidance, disposing of animals that had come to misfortune previously or accidentally. Whereas the idea of breeding orangs in captivity was almost unknown in zoos immediately after the Second World War, by 1964 some 13 per cent of those in listed zoos had been born in a cage. The latest available figure, for 1971, gives 539 orangs in zoos, of which 152 were born in captivity—a gratifying 28 per cent. The figure is still rising. However, one very serious problem still remains. Only a single recent birth has been reported between parents who were both themselves captive-bred.

One reason for this pseudo-sterility among captive orangs may well be the actual conditions under which they are kept. Although zoos generally have greatly improved in the past twenty years, these improvements have been notably less for the apes than for most other groups of animals. Larger houses and more sophisticated facilities have been provided for the gorillas, orangs, and chimpanzees—but they have been constructed with far less imagination than those for mountain goats, for example, or nocturnal animals, or dolphins, or fish. The new ape houses in the usually admirable London Zoo are a good example. They are wonders of architecture, concrete, and steel. But they are anathema to the way of arboreal life of the orang-utan, the jungle equivalent of a lifetime in Death Row.

There is in fact real and continuing cruelty to orangs even in good zoos. They cannot manage, psychologically and spiritually, with the same conditions as the largely terrestrial gorillas and chimpanzees. They are essentially wild men *of the trees*—who never see a green leaf. In the wild they are living enwrapped in greenery all the year round, in everlasting equatorial rainforest verdure.

The indiscriminate orang catching has not really been stabilized. Babies are still being illegally transported, primarily in small coastal vessels from Sumatra and Kalimantan (Indonesian Borneo) to Taiwan, and from there by air, especially to the Low Countries. A new difficulty is that they are being traded under the guise of having been 'captive-bred' in the dealers' own private zoos! But the overall situation *has* improved in the last fifteen years. Here perhaps, at the risk of being thought egocentric, I might quote from a report by a young Oxford scientist, John MacKinnon:

'Tom and Barbara Harrisson have made great efforts in

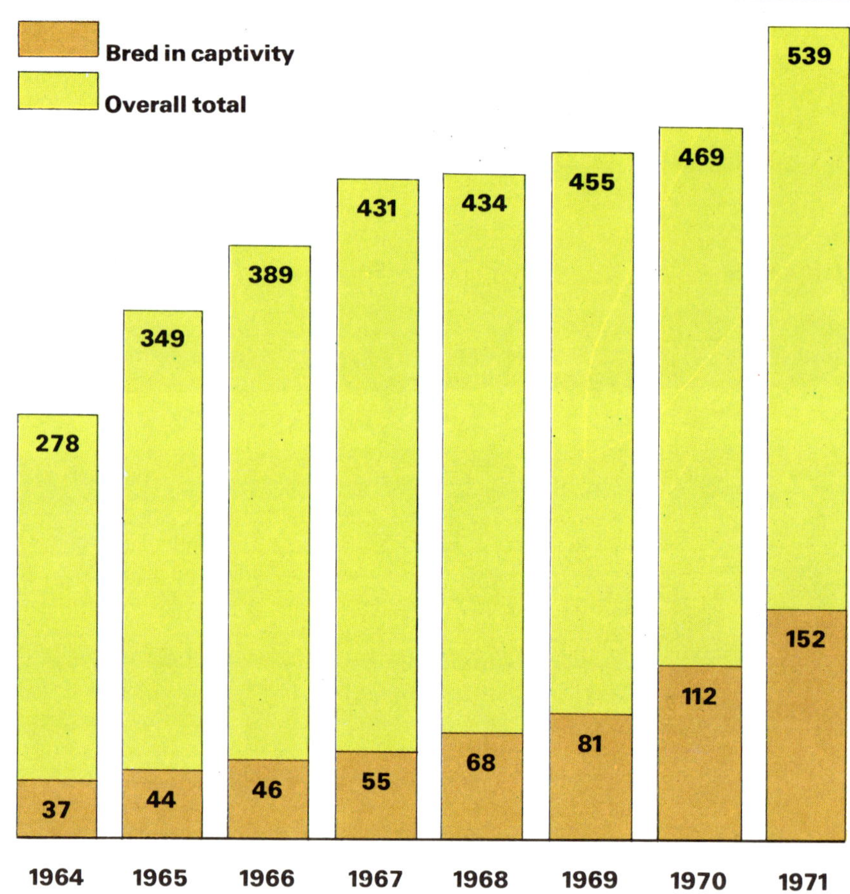

Orang-Utans in world zoos

the last fifteen years to bring to people's notice the plight of the orang-utan, and the steps that have been taken to protect orang-utans have been largely due to their efforts. In most countries in the world it is illegal to ship orang-utans, offer them for sale, or buy them. Thanks to international goodwill and co-operation it has become difficult to export orang-utans illegally from the Far East; all animal crates at Singapore and Hong Kong are checked by Customs. There is a census in operation of all animals in zoos, and any recent orang-utan acquisitions are traced. On top of this the animals are now protected in both Indonesia and Malaysia. It is illegal to kill or capture orang-utans or to keep one as a pet. Large areas of jungle have been laid aside as forest reserves where the cutting of timber is forbidden, thus protecting the orang-utan's habitat.

'Nevertheless, orang-utans are still being killed for their babies, which are sent falsely labelled, only to be intercepted by customs at Singapore or Hong Kong.'

John MacKinnon made his report at the end of 1970. But already he and others were noting a disturbing new trend. Both in Borneo and to a lesser extent Sumatra the economic pressures of under-development were pushing but when the pressure of national development comes into play, enlightenment has a hard time (as we in the developed world know only too well, from numerous examples in our own countries). An additional factor is that in areas like South-East Asia there is, so far, no informed mass of educated public opinion to support the enlightened politicians.

In Indonesia the situation had taken a still more serious turn, and quite suddenly. The new policy of the Indonesian government under President Suharto has been for a time to give huge timber concessions to outside companies and organizations, hitherto unwelcome. In particular, major tracts of land, including orang territory, have been granted to American and Japanese combines for immediate exploitation, both in Borneo (Kalimantan) and Sumatra. It is planned to quadruple timber production in the five years 1969 to 1974.

It is no good being unpleasant about these difficulties, no use blaming the local people. On the other hand, the problems must be faced. We are moving largely into the realm of politics, where conservation so often ends up; science no longer carries much weight at that level. In addition, even if the very top people mean well and make useful promises, their implementation lower down the economic scale is very hard to enforce.

And so, today, habitat destruction is the growing threat to the orang-utan. It is, incidentally, threatening a wide range of other species not even officially considered as threatened species at the moment. It may transform the pattern of the rainforests within the next few decades—so rapid are the new methods being deployed in timber extraction. The needs, the problems, of the under-developed nations are serious. It is easy to see their point of view. But we, as conservationists, must ceaselessly fight for the point of view of the orang, the silent, speechless ape, who has neither elected representative nor dictator. It is hard going. But it is not desperate going. It just requires the maximum of positive support for intelligent analysis of the problem and effective action to solve it.

At the worst, there are now enough orangs in the world's zoos almost to ensure breeding reservoirs, of a kind. But these animals are being bred under such wretched conditions in relation to the wild state that we are no longer getting 'real' orangs.

If only the orang could adapt itself more readily to changes in the Asian environment. Some have suggested that it can adapt to secondary jungle and lower scrub formation, but our observations suggest that this is wishful thinking. The orang-utan is so highly adapted to an advanced form of arboreal life, that it is truly the 'man of the jungle' in the Malay sense. It depends on highly complicated ecological relationships. It is especially sensitive to any tampering with the environment—and in that respect the opposite of modern man, who has evolved to the other extreme (with end results which may not yet be so different).

Baby orangs clamber over their Sea Dayak keeper at the rehabilitation center at Sepilok in the state of Sabah (North Borneo). Here they are re-trained in the ways of the wild.

the governments towards an ever-increasing exploitation of their greatest and superficially easiest natural asset—forest timber.

Throughout Indonesia and Malaysia the so-called 'virgin forests' are losing that particular status. Virginity no longer seems to be an asset. In Sabah, for instance, hill areas which appeared completely inaccessible to timber interests twenty years ago can now be entered with modern machinery and techniques. It is the declared policy of the government to exploit the timber resources as quickly as reasonably possible, in order to advance the living standards of the people of the state. Even the Sepilok Reserve, small as it is , is threatened by surrounding encroachment right now. The Sabah government has an extremely enlightened conservation policy;

27

David Stonegate

The Polar Bear–A Brighter Future

The polar bear, the great predator of the Arctic, could have vanished because governments refused to believe the best estimates of conservationists. As with so many other animal species, the experts began to see the warning signs of a serious decline in numbers before they had accumulated precise figures. All they had were their own 'guesstimates'—but the lawmakers disagreed with the experts for too long (what information did *they* have, to support their disagreement?), and nearly moved too late in passing measures to regulate polar bear hunting. Fortunately, they have at last begun to pay attention to the scientists' warnings, and the ice bear may be in for a new lease of life.

One of the largest members of the bear family, the polar bear weighs from 700 to 1,000 pounds (occasional big males can reach 2,000 pounds or more). It is a circumpolar animal, wandering the coasts and pack ice of, and off, the United States, Canada, Greenland, Spitzbergen, Norway, and the Soviet Union. Though polar bears rarely occur in the zone of permanent polar ice, they have been seen as far north as 88°; occasionally they will penetrate as far as a hundred miles inland. Normally almost entirely carnivorous, polar bears prey largely on the various seals found in the Arctic, especially the ring seal. However, recent research by a Canadian student has shown that in the Hudson Bay area, island populations feed mainly on seabirds in the summer and fall, while in the same period mainland bears eat large quantities of both land and marine vegetation.

Polar bears are solitary animals, and tend to come together only to mate, some time between March and May. About October the female retires to a maternity den she has dug out of the snow. The young—normally twins, one of each sex—are born in December, and leave the den with their mother in the spring. (Adult males also build dens in the winter, but these are only places in which to seek refuge in bad weather.) The following winter is also spent in the den with the mother, who eventually leaves them the next summer, when they are about twenty-one months old. The female will not mate again until the year after. Although the females are sexually mature when they are three, and remain fertile until the age of twenty-five, the fact that they breed only once in three years is a reason why the species is vulnerable to excessive hunting pressure.

The polar bear has few natural enemies. Walruses certainly take some, and it is possible that killer whales occasionally take their toll. Wolves, too, may account for a few, as may other polar bears when sufficiently hungry. But undoubtedly the main predator on the polar bear is man. For centuries past the Eskimos have hunted it, though there was probably no serious reduction (if any) in its overall numbers until the whaling ships ventured into the Arctic in the seventeenth century. The decline built up gradually, and although there are no estimates of the animal's original numbers, it is clear that it is now reduced to a fraction of its former abun-

Polar bears at Kong Karl's Land, Spitzbergen, a principal denning area. It is now a nature reserve.

29

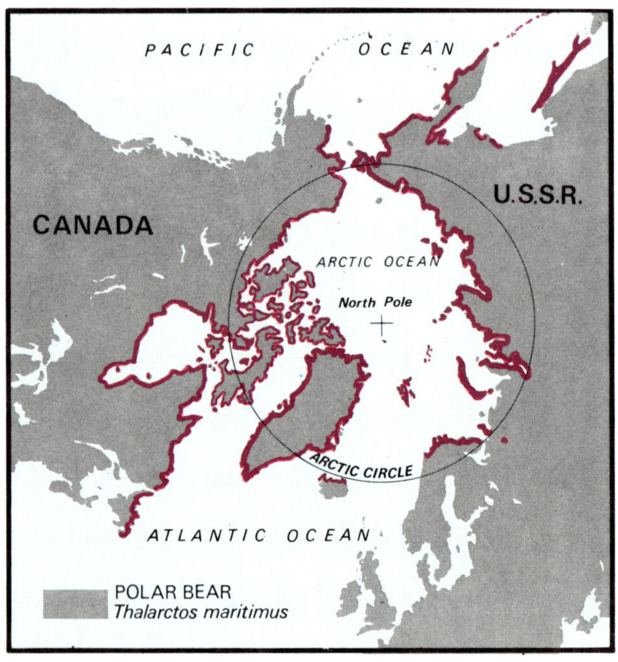

dance. The best current estimate is that there are between 10,000 and 20,000 polar bears still inhabiting the Arctic.

The principal cause of the decline in numbers is intensive hunting, either for pelts or for trophies. A particularly undesirable modern development has been the introduction of 'sport' hunting using light aircraft. As Shawn Christoph writes in *National Parks Magazine*: 'From Alaska light planes fly out in pairs over the international ice to locate a bear. The plane carrying hunter and guide lands, and the second plane stays aloft to see if they have trouble landing. Too often the second plane herds the bear towards the hunter.' Off Norway and Spitzbergen, hunters worked from shipboard with rifles, or with set guns. Canadian Eskimos are reportedly catching large numbers of bears with the aid of snow-mobiles.

Aside from hunting, it is thought that the range of the polar bear has been declining due to the onset of milder weather conditions in the Arctic in the past hundred years. Yet another adverse factor is the expansion of human beings, with their livestock, northwards into the arctic, leading to a higher incidence of disease.

Little is yet known about the biology of the polar bear, or its migratory habits, but the research effort is being stepped up. First the bears are located from the air (left), and then the animals are immobilized with a tranquilizer dart (right). This technique requires skill, but if carried out by experts is quite safe for both them and the bears. The animals are clearly marked (below left). so that they will be readily identifiable again from the air. Various scientific data are obtained, including the animals' weight (below right).

There are large gaps in our knowledge of the polar bear's ecology. Besides not knowing precisely how many animals there really are, we do not know enough about their migratory habits, nor how they survive Arctic conditions. The migrating patterns are important, because although bears have been protected for some years in the Soviet Union, it is believed that over-hunting in Norwegian and American territory has been 'made up' by animals moving in from the Soviet Arctic. The Russians have complained—with some justification—that they have been protecting the bears merely to provide more hunting for everyone else.

Interesting research methods have been used, or proposed, in the constant effort to find out more about the polar bear. Animals have been immobilized with tranquillizer drugs, tiny radio transmitters have been fitted to collars around their necks, and good results have been obtained in tracking them from aircraft. A program to track polar bears in Alaska from an orbiting polar satellite was submitted to NASA for funding, but never went into operation due to lack of funds. Likewise, a promising plan to follow bear movements with airborne infra-red (heat-sensing) equipment was interrupted due to budgetary limitations within the US Bureau of Sport Fisheries and Wildlife.

Despite these setbacks, information on the polar bear has steadily accumulated from year to year. Surveys are being made of den sites, and progress is being made in the development of census techniques. As already mentioned, the global bear population is thought to be between 10,000 and 20,000. In 1969–70 some 1,300 were killed, although this figure had dropped to about 900 in 1970–71, the latest year for which figures are available. Nevertheless, this is quite likely far too high an annual offtake.

Though government officials, especially in the United States and Norway, seem to have disagreed with the experts' assessments of the polar bear's status, at last the message is beginning to sink in, and solid conservation action is being taken. Once every two years polar bear scientists from Canada, Denmark, Norway, the Soviet Union and the United States meet under the sponsorship of the International Union for Conservation of Nature and Natural Resources (IUCN). At their fourth meeting, in Switzerland in 1972, they reported good progress, and called for a ban on all hunting of polar bears in international waters.

The Soviet Union has led the way in polar bear conservation, having banned all hunting since 1956. The United States reduced the annual Alaskan quota for trophy hunters to 300 in 1971, and at the same time reduced the former unlimited bag for residents who hunt from the ground and use polar bears for food, to three per hunter. Best news of all is that the Alaska Department of Fish and Game completely prohibited the use of aircraft for taking polar bears, as from July 1972. It is hoped that in Greenland a new National Park will be declared which will protect the main polar bear denning

areas, while in Canada polar bears are now totally protected along the Labrador coast of Newfoundland. In Spitzbergen, where as many as 700 bears were killed in 1970—many by trap guns set by local miners to obtain profitable skins—the Norwegian Government has announced a complete ban on killing bears for five years after the 1972–3 season, during which a quota of eighty-five has been allowed to local residents. Trap guns have already been banned. In 1971 a nature reserve was declared for three years on Kong Karls Land. A spring survey in 1972 showed this to be the main denning area in the Spitzbergen archipelago, and conservation organizations have appealed to the Government to make the reserve permanent. They have also asked the Government to establish reserves in other biologically important areas in accordance with its responsibilities under the 1921 Svalbard (Spitzbergen) Treaty, in the light of the dangers of current oil exploration and possible future exploration. One problem which will arise out of the reduction in polar bear hunting is a corresponding reduction in the number of recoveries of marked bears. New kinds of tags will thus have to be designed that will be visible on live animals.

The 1972 meeting resulted in a strong call to governments to ban all hunting of polar bears on the high seas

*Two young bears in the Russian arctic **(left)**, where they have been protected from hunting since 1956. The polar bear skins **(right)** are drying in the sun at Tromsö, Norway.*

from 1973 onwards. The only exception would be for continuation of hunting by local people traditionally dependent on the bears. The polar bear specialists were expected to put the finishing touches to a protocol to this effect in September 1972, which would also include protection of denning and feeding areas within national territories. The protocol is envisaged as an interim measure until an international convention on the conservation of polar bears can be approved.

So the polar bear survives, though much reduced in numbers. By refusing to take action until all the facts were in, governments nearly left it too late (as it is, they have only just moved ahead of another new threat that is looming for the polar bear, posed by the influx into Alaska of personnel involved in construction of the oil pipeline). But now with annual harvests dropping, and conservation regulations being tightened up, the big white bear is hopefully headed for a recovery.

Janet Barber

The Giant Panda

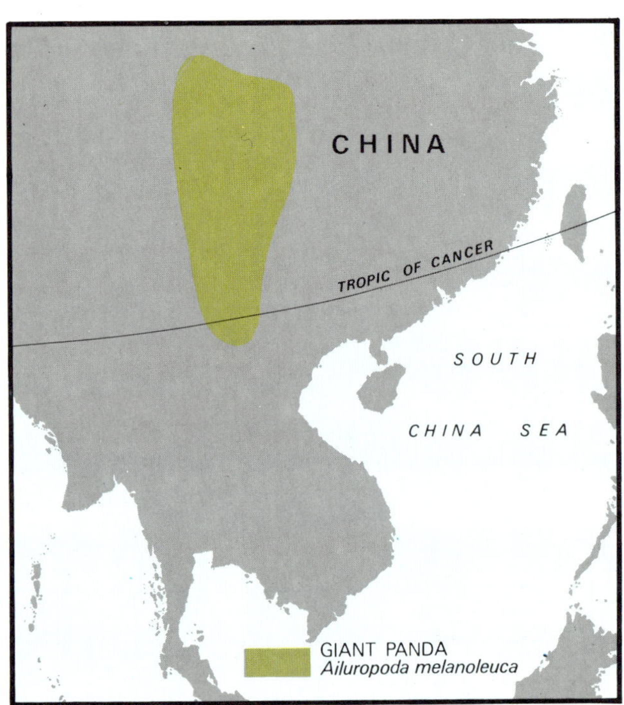

With the sad death of Chi-Chi at the London Zoo in July 1972, only three giant pandas now exist outside China—An-An in the Moscow Zoo, with whom Chi-Chi had an unsuccessful love affair, and the two pandas Ling-Ling and Hsing-Hsing at the National Zoological Park in Washington, DC. This pair, presented by the Chinese Government to the United States early in 1972, are the first giant pandas to live in the US since the death in 1953 of Mei-Lan at Brookfield Zoo, Chicago.

So although American panda hunters and collectors played a major role in stimulating the intermittent panda fever which has gripped the world during the last century, for nearly twenty years there was no live specimen in the country. Now Ling-Ling and Hsing-Hsing, seen as symbolizing a new and welcome trend in diplomatic relations between East and West, are generating renewed enthusiasm at a time when the British are mourning the death of perhaps the best loved and most famous panda of all, Chi-Chi.

The giant panda was unknown to the Western world until 1869 when the studious French priest Père Armand David, who had suspected the existence of a strange black and white bear in China, came across a skin. Refreshing himself with tea and sweet-meats in a remote valley in western China, while on a collecting trip for the Paris Museum of Natural History, he noticed the skin in the house of a local man. His belief that the species 'must constitute an interesting novelty for science' can only be described as an understatement. When skins of the new species finally reached Paris, the argument about the giant panda's place in the animal kingdom began. From its external characteristics, Père David had decided that it was likely to be related to the bears. But on detailed examination of the skins and skeletons Professor Alphonse Milne-Edwards said it must be related to the red panda, discovered earlier in the same century, and the raccoon family.

It is easy to understand why the giant panda had remained for so long undiscovered by westerners. Its territory is the most inhospitable of country in western Szechwan and eastern Sikang. Here steep-sided mountains, thickly covered with dripping forest, rise to snow-capped or mist-enshrouded peaks 17,000 feet high; the panda's range lies between 5,000 and 10,000 feet, or within the limits of the bamboo forests. No one but a zealous naturalist or hunter would be tempted to explore such terrain—and he would only be inspired to do so if he was in search of a particular specimen.

Following Père David's discovery there was something of a lull before others began to follow in his footsteps. A trip to Szechwan was not to be taken lightly. Costs were high and it is unlikely that even hardened explorers would have relished the prospect of pursuing the giant panda in China's often bandit-ridden interior.

The most difficult route into panda country was via Burma and thence north-west to Szechwan, and this was

Hsing-Hsing and Ling-Ling, the pair of giant pandas presented to President Nixon by the Chinese early in 1972, quickly pushed the White House into second place among Washington's tourist attractions. This is the male Hsing-Hsing, the less extrovert of the pair. Both are settling down well in their new quarters in the National Zoological Park.

Giant panda with young in the Peking Zoo, China. The only giant pandas known to have been born in captivity have been born in Chinese zoos.

GIANT PANDAS
IN CAPTIVITY OUTSIDE CHINA AND KOREA

Name	Sex	Final zoo home	Zoo life	Estimated total longevity
Su-Lin	m	Chicago	1937–38	1 year 6 months
Mei-Mei	m	Chicago	1938–42	5 years 3 months
Mei-Lan	m	Chicago	1939–53	14 years 8 months
Pandora	f	New York	1938–41	3 years 6 months
Pan	m	New York	1939–40	1 year 11 months
Pan-dee	f	New York	1941–45	4 years 7 months
Pan-dah	m	New York	1941–51	10 years 8 months
Happy	m	St Louis	1938–46	8 years 9 months +
Pao-Pei	f	St Louis	1939–52	13 years 7 months
Ling-Ling	f	Washington	1972–	1 year +
Hsing-Hsing	m	Washington	1972–	1 year +
Ming	f	London	1938–44	6 years 10 months
Tang	m	London	1938–40	2 years 10 months
Sung	m	London	1938–39	2 years 6 months
Grandma	f	London	1938–39	1 year 8 months
Lien-Ho	f	London	1946–50	4 years 4 months
Chi-Chi	f	London	1958–72	15 years 3 months
Ping-Ping	m	Moscow	1957–61	6 years 0 months +
An-An	m	Moscow	1959–72	15 years 1 month

London Zoo's Chi-Chi during a visit to Moscow—an unsuccessful attempt to get her to breed with the Russian's male panda, An-An.

the one chosen by the famous Roosevelt expedition of 1928. After various deceptions by local people and a long search, Theodore and Kermit Roosevelt, whose declared aim was to shoot a giant panda, came across one sleeping in the bole of a tree. As he roused himself and sleepily made off, both brothers fired and claimed the same victim simultaneously. They were greeted with great excitement on their return to the United States, and their panda was eventually mounted in Chicago, with another panda shot later. Inevitably, other museums were filled with the collecting zeal, and in 1934 Dean Sage Jr. led a party to China which managed to shoot an elderly nursing female. Its skin was in due course triumphantly presented to the American Museum of Natural History.

And then the search turned towards obtaining a live panda—not due to sentiment or conscience, but probably because it presented a greater challenge. In December 1936 Mrs Ruth Harkness, a New York dress designer, returned to San Francisco with an enchanting baby panda called Su-Lin. Finally established at the Brookfield Zoo, Chicago, Su-Lin was universally adored until she died just over a year later with a piece of wood stuck in her throat. So much impact did she make that for a while she even ousted the exploits of Al Capone from the front pages.

Next to come out of China was a colorful character named Floyd Tangier Smith, a keen rival of Mrs Harkness. He brought with him no less than five giant pandas. One, Ming, was to do for Britain what Su-Lin had done for the United States. The country was ecstatic. Baby Ming's magic drew the Royal Family to visit her, as well as soldiers on leave and thousands of adoring Londoners. When she died in 1944 she rated an obituary in *The Times*. Other pandas were acquired by American zoos, and another by London, but the next most famous was the celebrated Chi-Chi, who arrived in London in 1958.

In 1961, when the World Wildlife Fund was formed, a giant panda was chosen as its symbol. The animals were unmistakable, universally popular, and very rare. And above all, the giant panda is probably one of the few large rare animals that has a good chance of survival. More than sixteen giant pandas are thought to exist in Chinese zoos, and Peking Zoo began the successful breeding of pandas in 1963. The giant panda is strictly protected in the Szechwan mountains, and the existence of the *bei-shung*, as the Chinese call him, is something of which they are immensely proud.

The giant panda symbol designed by British naturalist Peter Scott now represents the World Wildlife Fund, and thus stands for wildlife conservation, in some eighteen different countries.

Madagascan villagers regard the aye-aye as an evil omen, and persecute it. It is endangered.

The Threatened Lemurs

The Bawean Deer Breeds

The Vicuna Recovers

Robert Martin

The Threatened Lemurs

The most primitive of all the living primates are the lemurs, which live only on the large island of Madagascar. Virtually all of them are threatened with extinction, some of them very seriously. While many animal species are endangered today, and conservationists hesitate to make value judgements on the relative importance of saving particular species, it is nevertheless true to say that the lemurs are more interesting to the scientist than a great many other creatures. They deserve a high conservation priority.

Two hundred million years ago, the island of Madagascar was probably attached to the African mainland. At that time the land-masses now known as South America, Africa, Madagascar, India, Australia, and Antarctica were apparently all joined together in one enormous southern supercontinent—Gondwanaland. This major land-mass was gradually fragmented by rifting, and the individual continents separated through continental drift. It seems likely that Madagascar was definitively separated from the mother-continent of Africa about 100 million years ago, and that its present position was reached about 20 million years ago. The island—a huge fragment of the continental plate, measuring approximately 1,000 miles by 350 miles—is now well separated from Africa by the Mozambique Channel, which is 250 miles wide at its narrowest point.

This long history of Madagascar is crucial to an understanding of the origins of the many unusual plants and animals which now occur there. Evolution is a slow process of change leading to the emergence of new life forms, and one of the main steps involved is the division of an ancestral species population to form two or more 'daughter' populations or species (speciation). The basic unit of evolution is the species (a single, interbreeding population), and it is widely recognized that the process of division to form new species depends upon the presence of some kind of geographical barrier to interbreeding. The break-up of the supercontinent Gondwanaland provided many new opportunities for speciation, since the new continents were separated by gradually widening water barriers. At one time, the plant and animal populations of Madagascar were continous with those of Africa; but as the island drifted away, separate populations were gradually formed. Madagascar was like a giant Noah's Ark, carrying off a sample of the organisms which inhabited Africa tens of millions of years ago. At first, some organisms could still emigrate from Madagascar to Africa. This became increasingly difficult, however, and nowadays the island can only be successfully invaded by organisms which can swim, float, or fly across the Mozambique Channel. Apart from these few new arrivals, the animals and plants of Madagascar are generally unique; nine-tenths of the species occur nowhere else in the world, and there are whole families of organisms which occur only on Madagascar.

For the biologist, therefore, Madagascar is like an immense laboratory of evolution. There is a vast amount to be learnt from studying life forms which have developed on islands near a major continent. Indeed, it was the range of unusual species on the Galapagos Islands off South America that helped Charles Darwin to formulate his theory of evolution in the nineteenth century. Animals or plants which manage to invade an island by chance subsequently develop in isolation, gradually becoming more and more distinct from their mainland relatives. This has applied many times over in Madagascar, especially since the island is so large and varied that evolution can continue quite rapidly within its boundaries. Thus the biological interest of Madagascar is twofold: the animals and plants are derived from stocks which once existed on the major continents (mainly Africa), and they have continued to evolve through the formation of new species on the island itself. However, because Madagascar is so isolated and so small relative to the main continents, evolution has progressed at a fairly leisurely pace without the added spur of competition of numerous more advanced forms arriving from other areas. For this reason, the organisms on Madagascar have generally remained rather primitive, and they can thus provide us with clues about early ancestral forms.

The preservation of relatively primitive forms on Madagascar is particularly important when one considers the mammals. When Madagascar was in the process of separating from Africa, the placental mammals were rapidly diversifying to replace the reptiles which had previously been dominant. As a result, a number of early mammal stocks—insectivores, primates, rodents, and carnivores—managed to invade Madagascar and establish themselves. The descendants of these four

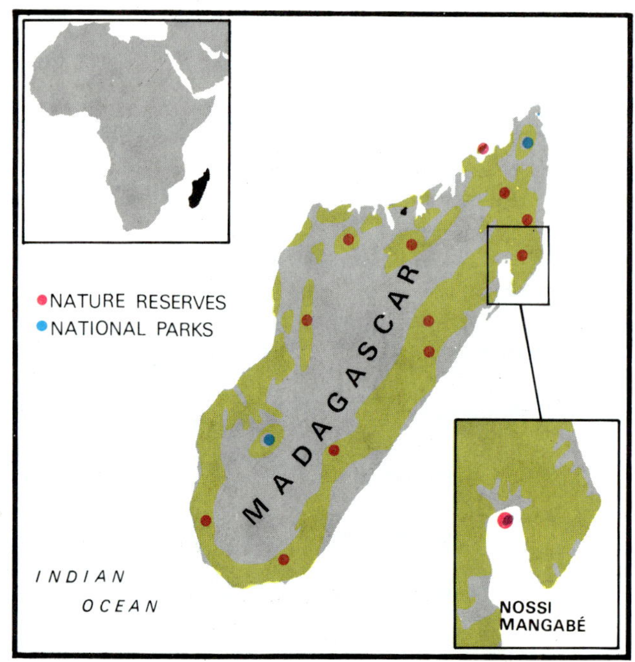

The aye-aye **(near right)** occurs in restricted coastal areas in the northern rainforest; it was believed extinct until 1957. Its elongated middle fingers are used to extract larvae from bark.

The fork-crowned lemur **(far right)** is only known from the west and north of Madagascar, and is probably rare. It is a small, nocturnal species.

Coquerel's sifaka **(near right)** is one of four species which have a very specialized form of locomotion known as 'vertical-clinging-and-leaping'. It is active by day and quite rare.

The brown lemur **(far right)** is widespread in Madagascar, but various local subspecies are restricted in distribution and their numbers are dwindling rapidly.

stocks can now provide us with information about the early evolution of the mammals. The Malagasy tenrecs (insectivores) possess many characters which were probably present in the ancestral stock that gave rise to all the placental mammals.

Even more important, however, are the lemurs. These mammals belong to the zoological order called the primates, along with the bushbabies, lorises, tarsiers, monkeys, apes, and man himself. The lemurs are the most primitive of the surviving primates, and they can therefore tell us a great deal about the evolution of the stock which eventually gave rise to man. Thus the conservation of lemurs in Madagascar is not simply a question of preserving a particular group of animals for future generations; it is also a question of preserving vital evidence relating to the evolution of man. Of course, all animals and plants are related through the framework of evolution, and conservation of any species means the preservation of a unique population occupying a place in that framework. On Madagascar, however, almost every living organism, because of its primitive characters, occupies a key place in evolutionary history. In the case of the lemurs, this key position concerns our own evolutionary heritage. The lemurs still show a remarkable similarity to primitive primates, known from fossils, which occurred in North America, Europe, Africa, and probably Asia 50 million years ago. If the lemurs were to become extinct, we would lose not only a valuable part of our natural inheritance, but also one of our most important links with our own past.

It is highly probable that the lemurs now found on Madagascar are all derived from a single ancestral stock which became established on the island at an early stage in its history. This stock gradually diversified to produce the nineteen species surviving today and at least fourteen recently extinct species, which are known almost exclusively from bones in museums. Each of these species developed within the island to occupy a particular ecological niche.

The lemurs have produced such a variety of forms within Madagascar for two main reasons. In the first place, there are relatively few competitors, and the lemurs have evolved to fill niches which are filled by other animals in other areas of the world. Secondly, the forests of Madagascar are so varied that the lemurs have been able to adapt to different habitat conditions in different parts of the island. Physical barriers—such as rivers and mountain ranges—have led to the formation of different species in these separate habitat areas. The variety of vegetation is itself based on variation in climatic factors (essentially rainfall and temperature) throughout the island. Trade-winds from the south-east give rise to heavy rainfall on the relatively hot east coast area, and this part of the island is accordingly covered with lush, tropical rainforest which is richest at its northern extreme. The land rises abruptly from the coast to a large, central plateau which is between 2,500 and

CURRENT STATUS OF LIVING LEMURS

Species	Status	● Listed in Red Data Book
Lesser mouse lemur *Microcebus murinus*	Relatively common	
Coquerel's mouse lemur *Microcebus coquereli*	Quite rare	●
Brown dwarf lemur *Cheirogaleus major*	Quite common	
Fat-tailed dwarf lemur *Cheirogaleus medius*	Quite rare	●
Fork-crowned lemur *Phaner furcifer*	Probably rare	●
Dwarf lemur *Allocebus trichotis*	Very rare—may be on verge of extinction	●
Ring-tailed lemur *Lemur catta*	Relatively common	
Brown lemur *Lemur macaco*	Various subspecies restricted in distribution, with numbers dwindling rapidly	●
Variegated lemur *Varecia variegata*	Not immediately threatened	
Red-bellied lemur *Lemur rubriventer*	Not immediately threatened	
Gray gentle lemur *Hapalemur griseus*	Precarious	●
Mongoose lemur *Lemur mongoz*	Not immediately threatened	
Broad-nosed gentle lemur *Hapalemur simus*	Precarious	
Sportive lemur *Lepilemur mustelinus*	Precarious	●
Avahi *Avahi laniger*	Quite rare	●
Verreaux's sifaka *Propithecus verreauxi*	Quite rare	●
Diadem sifaka *Propithecus diadema*	Quite rare	●
Indri *Indri indri*	Quite rare—probably fairly close to extinction	●
Aye-aye *Daubentonia madagascariensis*	Extremely rare, but now well protected on island reserve	●

5,500 feet above sea-level. The high altitude ensures relatively low temperatures throughout the year, whilst the trade-winds give rise to relatively high rainfall which supports mixed deciduous and evergreen forest with quite high humidity. Right along the west coast, there is a gradient of rainfall from north to south, and the region is marked by relatively hot deciduous forest with a marked annual rainy season. The annual rainfall decreases towards the south, where there is forest adapted for semi-arid, hot conditions. All of the plants have small leaves, thick fleshy appendages, or a combination of the two. In each of the main forest areas, there are lemur species adapted for the specific local conditions. The aye-aye, for example, is adapted to live in the richest, northern part of the east coast rainforest, while the ring-tailed lemur is adapted to live in the drier areas of the south.

For purposes of description, the living lemurs can be easily classified into four natural groups. The first contains the small, nocturnal mouse and dwarf lemurs, which generally have a diet of fruit, gums, and insects. The smallest of these—the lesser mouse lemur, which weighs less than 2 ounces—is still relatively common, and it occurs virtually anywhere where there is forest cover of some kind. If the lemurs do gradually become extinct, this will doubtless be the last species to disappear. However, a larger close relative, Coquerel's mouse lemur is quite rare, and may be in imminent danger of extinction. The brown dwarf lemur, which is just a little bigger than the red squirrel, is also quite common, but it is restricted to the east coast rainforest. In the drier areas, it is replaced by the fat-tailed dwarf lemur, which now seems to be quite rare. The fork-crowned lemur, which is just a little larger than the brown dwarf lemur, is only known from the west and the north of the island, and it is probably rare. Finally, there is the small-bodied dwarf lemur, which is known only from a few museum specimens and may be on the verge of extinction.

The second group of lemurs contains larger forms which range from the size of a cat to the size of a raccoon. The best known member of this group is the ring-tailed lemur, which is restricted to the south and south-west of Madagascar. This is a diurnal (active by day) species which forms quite large social groups containing about twenty individuals; it feeds mainly on fruits and some leaves. It is replaced in other areas by various subspecies of the brown lemur, which is crepuscular (active at dawn and dusk) in habits and forms smaller social groups of about half-a-dozen individuals. Although the brown lemur species is widespread, various local subspecies— such as Sandford's lemur (*Lemur macaco sandfordi*)— are extremely restricted in distribution, and their numbers are dwindling rapidly. In the east coast rainforest, there are two more crepuscular, mainly fruit-eating species which are still fairly widely distributed and are not immediately threatened with extinction: the varie-

43

gated lemur and the red-bellied lemur. The group of lemurs also contains three somewhat smaller species which feed primarily on leaves. Two of them are crepuscular in habits—the gray gentle lemur and the broad-nosed gentle lemur—whilst the other, the sportive lemur is nocturnal. All of these species are listed in the *Red Data Book*, and their situation is precarious. The gray gentle lemur and the sportive lemur have a wide potential distribution in the island, but the broad-nosed gentle lemur is only known from a restricted area of the east coast rainforest. Until recently, it was widely feared that this latter species might have disappeared for good; but Dr Jean-Jacques Petter not long ago discovered a small population in a forest area which is as yet relatively untouched.

A third group consists of four species which are essentially leaf- and fruit-eaters, and which exhibit a very specialized form of locomotion known as *vertical-clinging-and-leaping*. All of the other lemurs—except the sportive lemur, which also exhibits vertical-clinging-and-leaping—move by quadrupedal running most of the time. Members of this third group, however, leap between vertical trunks by thrusting off with their powerful hind legs and swinging around in mid-air to land feet-first. Between leaps, the animal rests on each trunk with the body held vertically. This kind of locomotion is of particular interest, since it was probably widespread among early primates. Among the living lemurs, it is best seen in the members of the third group; the nocturnal avahi, the two diurnal sifakes, and the diurnal indri. All four species are fairly large, ranging from the cat-sized avahi to the indri, which is the biggest of the lemurs and has the physique of a 10-year-old child. All of these vertical-clinging-and-leaping lemurs are quite rare. The indri, in particular, occurs only in the northern part of the east coast rainforest, and it is probably fairly close to extinction.

The fourth, and last, group of lemurs contains only one member—the aye-aye—which is so bizarre that it is placed in a group of its own. Its body is about as big as that of a fox, and it has coarse black fur, black membranous ears, and a bushy tail. Its two main peculiarities are the possession of an extremely thin middle finger on each hand and the presence of continuously-growing incisor teeth. The incisors are used to prize open bark and the kernels of fruit, whilst the thin fingers are used as probes to pulp and remove soft insect larvae and the fruit tissue. The aye-aye only occurs in restricted coastal areas in the northern part of the rain-forest, and it was actually believed to be extinct until 1957, when Dr Petter and his wife spotted two of these unusual animals in the course of an expedition. However, the aye-aye population is now extremely small, and only a concerted effort can save the species from extinction. Unlike the other lemurs, which are generally protected (at least to some extent) by local customs and the general belief that the lemurs are benevolent and harmless, the aye-aye

is regarded as an evil omen. If one is found near a village, the occupants will usually either abandon the village entirely, or kill the animal and bury it, or display it at the entrance to the village. In view of its nocturnal habits, its bizarre appearance, and its eerie, screeching calls, it is hardly surprising that the aye-aye is viewed with mistrust by the villagers. Hence the only reliable course for conservation is to seal off an aye-aye population in an area where it will not alarm them, and where it can be effectively protected.

All of the lemurs are threatened with extinction to some extent, however, and ultimately the question of their conservation becomes a question of preserving large areas of natural forest. This is not a matter of preserving one particular valuable species, but of preserving a whole range of valuable and unique habitats. At present, these habitats are threatened in various ways by the human population. Fire is extensively used in agriculture, partly for clearing forest areas for new cultivation and partly for burning off vegetation in order to produce fresh, green shoots for domestic animals. Apart from the fact that this practice eventually leads to irreparable damage to the soil, there are too many occasions when the fires break loose and ravage the forest refuge areas containing the lemurs. What was once a carpet of forest over Madagascar is now no more than a fragmented wreath around the coastline, and what little forest remains is decreasing in extent every year. Zebu cattle, goats, and pigs can rapidly destroy vegetation in marginal forest areas, and in the dry areas of the south it is often necessary to cut down trees to give cattle a few precious leaves as fodder. Timber is widely used for construction and as firewood, and the forest is gradually receding as the human population grows and makes increasing demands on areas of forest as yet untouched by destructive agricultural practices. The Malagasy government must naturally ensure that the human population has room to live and enough to eat, and without international aid it is unlikely that the country will be able to cope with the conflict between the needs of the human population and the vast problem of protecting representative areas of forest throughout the island.

The problem of forest-destruction was recognized quite early in Madagascar. Between 1927 and 1952, various decrees were passed to establish twelve nature reserves, and two National Parks were created in 1958 and 1962, respectively. In contrast to many nature reserves in other parts of the world, however, these forest areas were not primarily chosen to encourage tourism. They were deliberately selected to be as far as possible from areas with large human populations, and they tended to be in the most inaccessible parts of the island. Each area was chosen to preserve a whole range of plants and animals peculiar to the region. However, the very isolation of these reserves creates problems in their management, and it has prevented the Malagasy government from exploiting the tourist trade, which provides an

important source of income for conservation in many other countries. The government is only able to devote a small budget to maintaining and patrolling the reserved areas. The necessary laws and the goodwill are already available, but extensive international aid will be required to ensure successful conservation programs. In October 1970 an international conference on conservation and the utilization of natural resources was held in Tananarive, the capital of Madagascar. This conference adequately showed that the Malagasy government is committed to the conservation of the natural forest areas, and that the official responsible for forest management are prepared to do their utmost—often in the face of impossible odds—to preserve these areas and the lemurs they contain. Hopefully, the conference will also lead eventually to an increase in international funds to assist the government in conserving its unique flora and fauna.

The World Wildlife Fund and the International Union for Conservation of Nature (IUCN) have already contributed extensively to the conservation effort in Madagascar. Their aid has supported a program of research and surveying led by Dr Petter. Perhaps one of the most vital steps has been the establishment of a special island reserve for the protection of the aye-aye. After Dr Petter had discovered living aye-ayes in 1957, he was assisted by World Wildlife and IUCN in the capture of nine adult animals, which were transported to the island of Nossi Mangabé and released there. This island was declared a reserve area by the Malagasy government in December 1965; since then, it has been fairly easy to protect it from interference, and it is quite likely that the introduced aye-ayes will settle down and produce a thriving colony. Thus there is at least a fighting chance that the aye-aye will not join the ranks of the fourteen subfossil lemur species, which live on only in Malagasy mythology following their extinction through competition with the first human habitants, who reached the island only about 2,000 years ago.

*A female sifaka (**top**) carries her baby on her back. They leap between vertical trunks by thrusting off with their powerful hind legs and swinging around in mid-air to land feet-first.*

*Ring-tailed lemurs are (**left**) restricted to the south and south-west of Madagascar. They form quite large social groups containing about twenty individuals, and are not immediately threatened with extinction.*

45

Nigel Sitwell

The Bawean Deer Breeds

In 1969 I made an expedition to the little Indonesian island of Bawean in the Java Sea, some 125 miles north of the eastern end of Java. I was accompanying a team from the Surabaja Zoo, led by one of its directors, Hilmi Oesman. Our objective was to seek out the rare and little known Bawean deer—*Hyelaphus kuhlii*—which only lives on that one small island and nowhere else on earth. No one even knew if it still existed, as apparently no naturalist had visited the island for many years.

The Bawean deer is hardly mentioned in most reference books, and certainly is a little known species. It was 'discovered' in 1836 by Salomon Müller, who came across some of the animals in the garden of the governor of Tuban, a small town on the north coast of Java. It is a smallish deer about two feet tall at the shoulder, and is lightish teak-brown in color. It has a striking gait, best described as crouching, with the rump much higher than the shoulders. The antlers are slender and six-tined.

There is something of a mystery surrounding the Bawean deer, for it appears to be quite distinct from all the other deer in Indonesia, which either belong to the genus *Rusa* (sambar deer) or the genus *Muntiacus* (barking deer). I have followed the Dutch zoologist Van Bemmel in putting it into the genus *Hyelaphus*, but other scientists believe it should be in the genus *Axis*. At any rate, both these groups of deer are found only in continental Asia, a long way from the island of Bawean.

Without getting too technical, it seems that the Bawean deer is what is known as a relict species, and reached the island long ago in the past when the Sunda Shelf was above sea-level. This theory is supported by the fact that a fossil deer has been found in nearby Java that closely resembles it, and also by the fact that the common Asian species, the chital, also lived in Java a long time ago.

It was—and is—therefore an animal of great interest, and we were keen to find out its current status. We made a number of expeditions through the south-western quarter of the island, during which half a dozen animals were definitely seen, and ten were reportedly seen feeding by night in a rice paddy. Judging from our own observations and discussions with the islanders we reckoned that the number of deer on Bawean Island was probably about 500—though it could have been as many as 1,000 or alternatively much fewer.

This number may seem satisfactory for an island with an area of about eighty square miles, but it is not that many when one considers that it represents the total world population, and when one takes into account the 50,000 or more human beings who also live there. Originally the people lived around the coast, but as numbers increased, they have been forced to expand inwards. Consequently, the island's remaining forest (which is also the deer's habitat) is gradually disappearing

During the 1969 expedition two animals were collected —a young male (named 'Bulu') and a baby female ('Djati'). This was particularly exciting not only because

Young adult male Bawean deer discovered in captivity, perhaps a year old, with antlers just beginning to grow.

The author holding a three-month-old female Bawean deer— conclusive proof that the species still existed in the wild.

Female Bawean
deer (a rare
species) with her
newly born young
in Surabaja Zoo,
Indonesia.

of the previous doubt about their existence, but also because no more than a handful had ever before been kept in captivity. The two deer, which had in fact been discovered in captivity in villages on the island, were transferred to the Surabaja Zoo where they became the only two specimens in the world outside Bawean island.

The two rare animals grew to maturity under the watchful and dedicated eyes of the zoo's staff. Obviously everyone hoped that the two would breed, but although during the rut Bulu showed great interest, Djati never seemed to respond. And so 1970 went by without any further development. But then on 1 March 1971 another pair of Bawean deer were brought to Surabaja, with the help of the local authorities on the island. Both the buck ('Sangka') and the doe ('Puri') were young adults, and had like their predecessors been in captivity on the island, although in different villages. On arrival at the zoo they were thin and apparently underfed, but they soon gained weight and were additional cause for pride in the rare collection.

When the new arrivals were introduced to the older pair there was a change of partners. Bulu left Djati and paired with Puri, while Sangka joined Djati. The new pairings seemed well established, but months went by without any reports from the keeper about positive mating. But with the new year, 1972, came renewed hope. There appeared to be a noticeable change in the shape of both does, although the keeper had not observed any mating activity. And at last came the long-awaited event: during the night of 27 January 1972 Puri gave birth. The youngster—a female—was the first Bawean deer ever to be born in a zoo.

'Ida', as the new-born deer was called, was a miniature replica of her mother, except for a row of white spots on each side of her back. She started to suckle one day after she was born. Hardly had the excitement subsided when a second baby was born, on 6 February just before dawn. This time Djati, the first animal we collected in 1969, was the mother. 'Elsi' was also a female, and began to suckle during the second day of her life.

Finally, to add to the excitement, the zoo received another adult female on 20 February 1972. She had been caught by some islanders, but because she was badly wounded she was taken direct to the mainland zoo by the Forestry Department. Apparantly she was already pregnant when she arrived, for on 3 May she gave birth to a male fawn.

So now the captive stock of Bawean deer totals eight animals—three males and five females. This great success means that a breeding stock has been established of this rare species. Obviously it is hoped that more will be born in the years to come, and that the species will at least survive in captivity even if it should become extinct on its island home.

Hartmut Jungius

The Vicuna Recovers

When we speak of conservation and wildlife management we are inclined to think that both were invented in modern times. We forget, or perhaps we do not know, that wild animal species were protected by laws and well planned management long before the present century. The Indian emperor Ashoka defined that preservation of wildlife and forest trees are a king's duty and forbade the killing of many wild animals about 2,000 years ago. In Africa some antelope species such as the addax, scimitar-horned-oryx and the North African subspecies of the harte-beest were kept in semi-captivity by the ancient Egyptians and used for food or religious purposes. In South America the vicuna was commercially exploited on a sustained yield basis for its wool and skin by the Incas. The preservation of the vicuna is an excellent example of ancient conservation practices and when protecting the species today we are merely reviving a tradition which had lapsed for several hundred years.

Protected against harsh winds, hail, frost, and snow by its thick coat of fine wool, the vicuna, a small member of the camel family, lives only in the high Andes. It is found at heights of 11,000 to 14,500 feet, mostly beyond the tree line.

The first Europeans found vicunas in large numbers throughout the Andean plateaux and valleys from southern Ecuador to southern Chile. Within this region the habitats ranged from areas with sparse vegetation and scanty fresh water supplies to others abounding in water and a rich plant cover. Due to their enormous adaptability vicunas are able to live in the dry semi-deserts of southern Bolivia and northern Chile, and the bare gravel plains around the vast saltpans of Uyuni and Coipasa. In contrast, they also occur in the moist Peruvian *paramos* where fodder is abundant. They inhabit peatbogs formed by hard cushion plants and luxurious vegetation, and they frequent the rolling *Puna* grasslands from southern Peru to middle Chile with its typical tuft grasses.

This wide distribution pattern has been altered considerably by man, and today the vicuna's range is much restricted. The populations are no longer joined with one another, but isolated into small groups. Human activities, including the increase of domestic stock, have eliminated vicunas from most of their favorite grazing sites and forced them to retreat to the drier parts of their range. Everywhere the vicuna was threatened with extinction until a few years ago. But it was not always so.

The vicuna was an important natural source of wool, skins, and meat in the time of the Incas. A permanent supply was needed and so techniques were worked out to ensure its conservation. The vicuna was proclaimed part of the state religion and was worshipped as the daughter of Pachamama, the Goddess of Fertility. The animal was sacred and only the Incas were allowed to wear its wool. Killing a vicuna without permission was a state offense. Only the government authorities could organize vicuna hunts, which, although they took place throughout the species' range, were restricted to certain areas and held at intervals of three to five years. The animals used to be rounded up and after their wool had been taken, most of them were released. These provisions, plus a system of closed seasons for hunting, gave the best guarantee that vicuna populations were not over-exploited.

Unfortunately, this well established management plan was abandoned after the fall of the Inca Empire. Old laws were pushed aside, the religion was crushed, and results of several hundred years of effective conservation were nullified in a few decades. Tens of thousands of vicunas were killed indiscriminately every year, but it was a long time before anyone recognized that the species was threatened. In fact, it was Simon Bolivar, the great South American statesman and hero, who saw the danger and did something about it. Realizing that the vicuna was a traditional symbol for the newly established Andean states, he issued the first decree (in 1825) prohibiting the killing of the animal in Peru, and established the first modern conservation law of his continent. Later the vicuna was included in the Peruvian coat of arms and appeared on the country's coins. However, despite this and further protective laws in Peru and other countries the stocks continued to decline rapidly.

Vicunas were wantonly slaughtered for their skins and their wool until the middle of the twentieth century, so it is perhaps surprising that in 1950 there were still some 100,000 animals remaining from the original million-plus population. Even then it would not have been too late to establish a systematic management plan to maintain and then rebuild the surviving stocks. But the over-hunting went on, despite the conservationists' warnings,

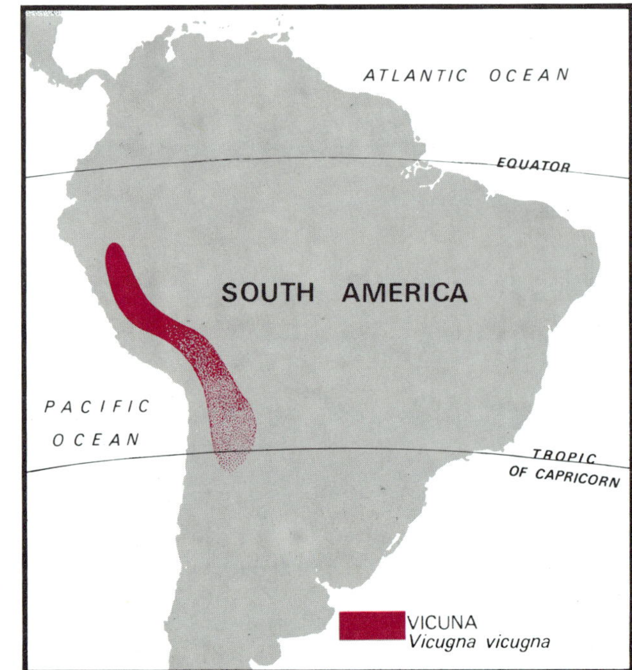

A small member
of the camel
family, the vicuna
lives only in the
Andes, above
11,000 feet.

51

and a few years ago the animal was almost wiped out.

The world's vicuna population reached its lowest level in the early 1960s. And then, in 1964, it was once more Peru which made history by initiating the establishment of the first vicuna reserve at Pampas Galeras which was officially proclaimed on 18 May 1967. Numbering some 1,000 animals at the time, the population in the reserve has now increased to more than 6,000, thanks to diligent protection. Some areas in the reserve, in fact, are already so densely populated that the vicunas leave the reserve and settle in surrounding areas. In addition it is planned to catch animals and reintroduce them to suitable habitats in other parts of the country. Peru leads its neighbors in vicuna conservation, and outside Pampas Galeras the animals are scattered throughout the country from latitude 9° 30′ N to its southern boundary, though in widely separated groups. The total population in Peru is about 15,000 (including the Pampas Galeras population).

The exact status of the species in Bolivia was unknown for a long time—in fact, until my own work there in 1969 and 1971. The largest concentrations of vicuna are now known to live along the Peruvian border north-east and south-west of Lake Titicaca. The largest group of vicunas in the country are the 200 to 250 animals to the north-east of the lake in the Pampa of Ulla Ulla. Together with my Bolivian colleagues I was also able to confirm the existence of small numbers in the Eastern Cordillera, around Lago Poopo and in the province of Lipez. We estimate that there are about 1,000 to 1,500 vicunas in the whole of Bolivia.

Until 1971 all the evidence from Chile and Argentina suggested that the vicuna was virtually exterminated in those two countries. But then, at the urging of World Wildlife and the International Union for Conservation of Nature and Natural Resources, local conservationists investigated the species' status more carefully during 1971 and 1972. It is impossible yet to give final details, but I am glad to say that I must withdraw my earlier pessimistic prediction that the vicuna had more or less disappeared in Chile and Argentina. From a preliminary survey undertaken by official bodies in both countries, as well as from observations by Jeffery Boswall, it is apparent that the vicuna still has a good chance of survival.

The southern limit of the species' distribution is latitude 29° S, between Vallenar (Chile) and La Riocha (Argentina), as indicated by Röhrs in 1957. This does not seem to have altered very much, and new data suggests that there are vicunas even to the south of this line. J. Rotmann estimates that there may be about 650 of the animals in Chile—200 to 400 in Tarapaca Province, 200 in Antofagasta Province, and 50 in Atacama Province. It is quite possible that more detailed surveys will show that the total is well in excess of 1,000.

The situation in Argentina is not so clear yet. D. J. Cutillo, Dirección Nacional de Recursos Naturales Renovables, estimates 2,000 vicunas in the province of San Juan in the south of the species, range. For the other provinces of north-western Argentina he gives the following figures: Salta 600, Juguy 800, La Rioja 800, Catamarca 1,000. Jeffery Boswall, a BBC Television producer, stayed in Jujuy and personally observed about 80 vicunas, and after discussions with the local people he reckons that the Argentine population can be measured confidently in hundreds of animals. According to the new information we may even estimate that several thousands occur.

Alarmed by the sharp decline of the vicuna, the IUCN included it in its *Red Data Book* of endangered species in 1969, and in 1971 called on all conservationists and scientists with a particular interest in the vicuna to join together and work out a plan to save the species from extinction. Thanks to financial help from the World Wildlife Fund it was possible to hold a meeting of this group in Lima in December 1971. The participants in this first international scientific conference on vicuna conservation included official delegates from Argentina, Bolivia, Chile, and Peru, and representatives of international governmental organizations, non-governmental organizations, and national organizations.

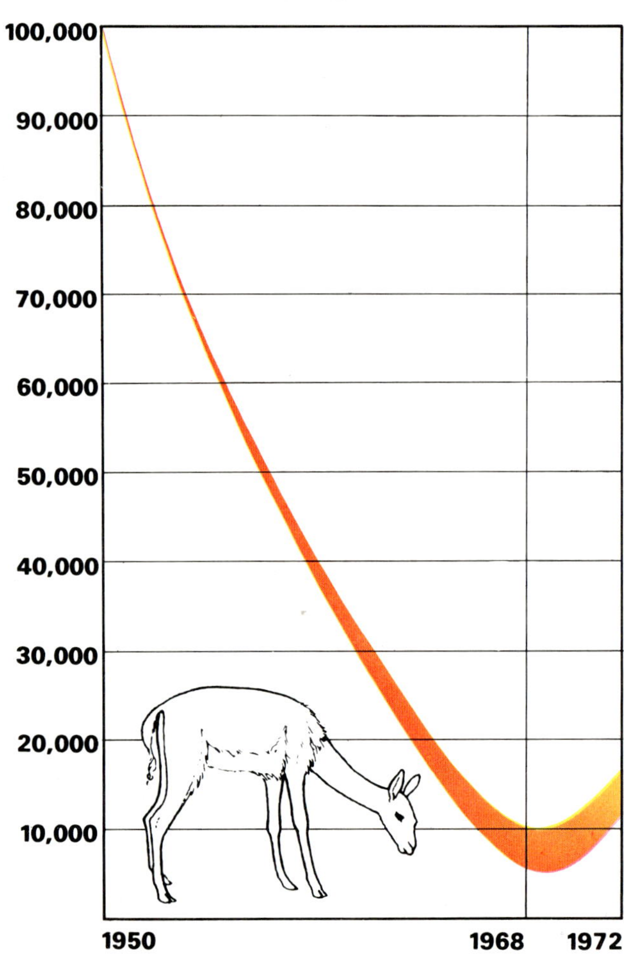

Vicuna population

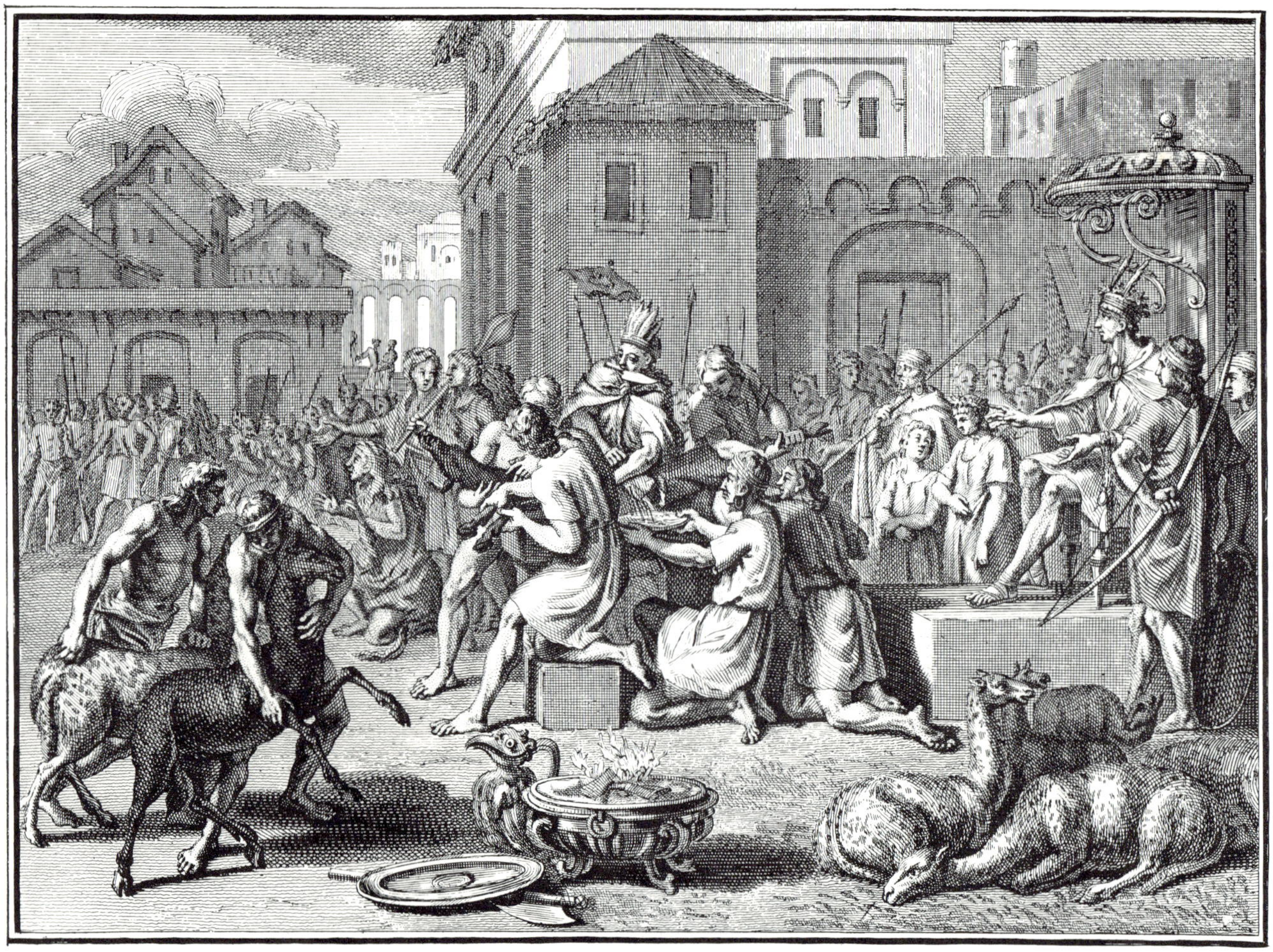

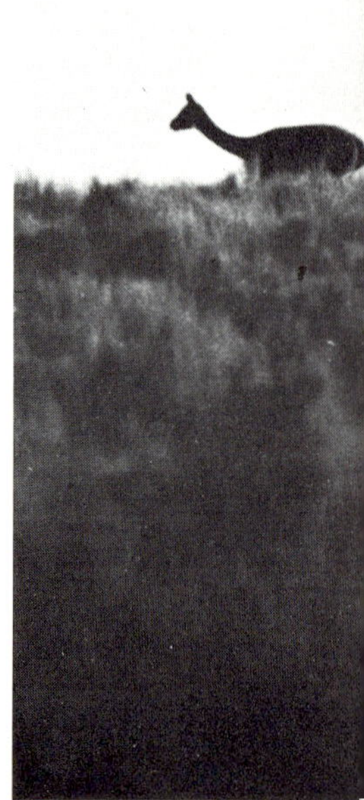

The conference took a close look at the problems faced by the species on a regional and international scale, and established guidelines for a conservation program. It initiated more research into vicuna biology and practical conservation; it created a wide interest in this animal in South American countries; and it established for the first time fruitful co-operation between the world's best known vicuna experts and the conservation authorities from the four vicuna countries.

The first objective of the overall program called for enforcement of the laws protecting the species in its natural environment. This was because one reserve (Pampas Galeras, Peru) is not enough to ensure the animal's survival. In 1970 Chile proclaimed the establishment of the Rio Lauca National Park in Tarapaca Province, which contains about 200 vicunas, and in 1971–72 the degree of protection was greatly up-graded by the establishment of a permanent guard post. In 1969 a UNESCO mission recommended that a reserve should be set up in the Pampa of Ulla Ulla.

Encouraged by World Wildlife and IUCN, the Bolivian Government has now legally proclaimed the area a reserve. Four game guards are constantly on patrol, thanks to equipment donated by the Frankfurt Zoological Society. Poaching has almost ceased, and the vicuna population has steadily increased from about 150 in 1969 to about 250 in 1972.

At the time of writing negotiations are under way between Peru and Bolivia to form an international reserve in the Ulla Ulla area. The World Wildlife Fund has raised funds to assist, and the Frankfurt Zoological Society has again promised its help. Under proper management, the area could become one of the most out-outstanding reserves in the Andes. Argentina investigated the species' status in more detail. In June 1972, a conference on vicuna conservation was held in San Juan and it was decided to establish the fourth reserve for this animal. It was encouraging to learn that resulting from the International Vicuna Conference's recommendations, plans are well advanced to proclaim the reserve 'San Guillermo' in this province of San Juan, which will cover some 10,000 square miles.

An interesting plan to improve the vicuna's prospects outside the reserves has been originated in Peru. The plan basically consists of setting up surveillance centers in areas with important vicuna populations. These

(Left) *An early impression of an Inca ceremony. The Incas worshipped the vicuna as the daughter of Pachamama, the Goddess of Fertility; only the Incas themselves could wear its wool. Because of its special position in their religion, the Incas worked out strict conservation measures—which were ignored when they were overthrown.*
(Above) *A small herd of vicuna high in the Peruvian Andes.*

centers consist of a guardpost occupied by two fully equipped guards. A network of such centers throughout the species' range would be the best provision for a rapid rebuilding of the populations. The centers can also serve as research stations, and later become centers for commercial vicuna management.

Protection of the vicuna in its natural habitat can only have long-term success if an awareness of its economic and cultural value can be created among the governments and peoples concerned. Accordingly, a vast educational campaign was planned in Peru and Bolivia in 1972. Peruvian and Bolivian conservationists were preparing booklets for school children and the general public. At the time of writing, posters and automobile stickers are being prepared appealing to the public to conserve this unique animal.

A major problem which has yet to be solved is the trade in vicuna products, especially wool. The demand from Western tourists and from developed countries, and the high prices paid, remain a compelling stimulus for the poacher. Great Britain and the United States have already banned the import of vicuna products: this is important progress, but it is still vital for other countries, especially France and Italy, to follow suit. However, as long as such goods are openly sold in Chile, Argentina, and particularly in Bolivia, despite legal prohibition, the incentive for poaching will remain. One way to halt this aspect of the trade is to educate tourists not to buy vicuna products. The World Wildlife Fund is therefore helping Peru and Bolivia prepare an information campaign aimed at foreign tourists.

If these three action programs—protection in the field, education, and the banning of trade—are successful, the vicuna will be saved, and we could be faced with a population explosion in the coming years. This will prove a tourist attraction and will also open the way for other activities, such as the reintroduction of vicunas into areas where they have been exterminated, and establishing management areas where they can be commercially exploited on a rational basis. R. Hofmann, a member of the Vicuna Group, is already working on such a plan in Peru, and we hope that it may be possible to announce in 1973 that the first populations are rationally utilized and that the first animals have been successfully reintroduced into places where their ancestors were slaughtered long, long ago.

Adult female peregrine falcon feeding her chick in an old raven's nest in the Scottish Highlands.

The Peregrine Falcon

West Indian Parrots

The Birds of the Seychelles

New Laws for Italian Birds

The Peregrine Falcon

Derek Ratcliffe

The Peregrine in Britain

The peregrine falcon has always had a special glamor in the world of wild creatures, but in recent years it has acquired a new symbolism, as a sensitive pointer to an especially insidious wasting of the richness of this world through man's thoughtless or uncaring activities. From its almost world-wide distribution and capacity for withstanding the more direct onslaughts of man, the peregrine has been reckoned among the most successful of all birds. The British Isles were one of its main European strongholds, with a population approaching 1,000 breeding pairs, well spread along cliff-bound coasts and amongst inland mountain crags. After at least a century of persecution by gamekeepers, pigeon-fanciers, and egg-collectors, its numbers in 1955 still came near this level. Yet by 1963 the peregrine population had crashed to about half its former strength, and many parts of continental Europe (and North America) reported even greater declines. Many of the remaining pairs failed to lay or broke their eggs, and the majority of peregrine eggs proved to be thinner shelled than usual. In these few short years the new, post-war upsurge in environmental contamination by synthetic toxic chemicals, especially the persistent organochlorine pesticides of agriculture, had done unprecedented damage to this once resilient bird of prey.

The suggestion that pesticides were largely to blame was vigorously challenged by those with a vested interest in these chemicals, and the circumstantial nature of the evidence has been attacked in particular. Nevertheless, many uncommitted scientists accept that the various lines of evidence, all pointing the same way, add up to a most persuasive argument—that the population decline of the peregrine was caused by the physiological effects of poisonous residues of these chemicals absorbed from contaminated prey. Most people agreed, however, that the most convincing confirmation of this case would be a recovery of peregrine numbers following closely on a substantial reduction in use of the chemicals believed to be responsible. As a result of pressure to reduce excessive pesticide use, and more especially from certain restrictions recommended by the British Government's scientific advisers, the amounts of organochlorine pesticides in circulation in the British environment have certainly diminished during the last decade. It was therefore felt that a repeat of the national census of peregrine breeding population during 1971 would be most timely. The census was again conducted by the British Trust for Ornithology, with support from the Nature Conservancy.

Gulls are often in conflict with aircraft at coastal airfields, and peregrines are used to keep the runways clear. Here Petty Officer White shows off his charge at the Royal Naval Air Station at Lossiemouth in Scotland.

The field work for the 1971 survey involved the concerted efforts of about 200 ornithologists, both amateur and professional, and through their enthusiasm it proved possible to examine 726 (90 per cent) of the 806 localities where peregrines have been known to breed since 1930. Peregrines were present in 340 of these localities, and this is estimated to be 54 per cent of the level which could have been expected in an average pre-1939 year. Many localities had pairs of peregrines, and of these 156 actually hatched young, corresponding to 25 per cent of the expected pre-war population. The peregrine population of Great Britain appeared to reach its lowest level in 1963, when numbers were estimated at 44 per cent, and hatching success at 16 per cent of the pre-war level. There has thus been a slight improvement in the situation nationally, matching the reduction in use of persistent pesticides. A separate survey by Irish ornithologists showed that in 1971 about 70 per cent of peregrine breeding stations in Ireland were occupied, and about 21 per cent of the pairs bred successfully.

The picture becomes more complicated when different parts of Great Britain are considered. The decline in numbers and breeding success began in 1956 in southern England and gradually spread northwards. By 1963 peregrines had been reduced to the merest handful in England, Wales, and southern Scotland (which together once contained about half the total British population), and most of the remaining birds were in the Scottish Highlands. In 1971 there was clear evidence of a recovery in numbers and breeding success in *inland* districts of northern England, southern Scotland, and the Highlands, but not in most coastal parts of these regions, nor in any part of Wales or southern England. In Shetland, numbers were even lower than in 1963.

Contamination of peregrines by toxic chemicals has been studied since 1963 by analyzing eggs (into which these substances pass) from northern England, southern Scotland, and the Highlands, and the levels of DDE (from DDT), dieldrin, heptachlor epoxide, and lindane have shown a downward trend in all inland districts here since 1966. It is interesting that the only part of Britain virtually unaffected by the recent decline (the central Highlands) has consistently shown the lowest chemical residues, and in this district peregrines have also laid thicker-shelled eggs, and less often broken these, than elsewhere. Despite the reduced use of pesticides, it is nevertheless clear that the amount of dieldrin seed dressing used in arable farming districts is a serious hazard to peregrines and probably causes the premature death of both adults and yearling birds. Pesticide risks, through feeding on contaminated prey, decrease with distance from arable districts, but there is a further problem in that peregrines in barren parts of the northern Highlands and islands may move in winter to areas of better food supply and may then come into closer contact with pesticides.

In addition, coastal peregrines often feed upon seabirds and then obtain a still wider range of toxic chemicals through marine food chains, including not only the organochlorine pesticides but also industrial pollutants such as the polychlorinated biphenyls (PCBs). The sea has become a general dump, collecting all manner of chemical wastes, and marine pollution is likely to be the main reason for lack of recovery in northern coastal districts.

With an annual total of around 300 young fledged in recent years, breeding success would seem good enough to allow steady recovery of the peregrine population to its 1955 level. It is probable, however, that chemical pollution greatly reduces the rate of recovery by increasing the risks of early death, and that the present state of the population, while representing an improvement, shows a new point of balance, with peregrine numbers still held well below their potential level by unfavorable conditions in many parts of the country. Whilst other more direct human activities, such as destruction by gamekeepers, taking of young for falconry, and disturbance by rock climbers, take their toll and could become serious, they are not at present really important. It seems much more likely that the fate of this fine bird, in Britain and elsewhere in Europe, will depend more on the future chemical situation. Conservationists can take heart that their efforts have retrieved what once seemed a disastrous situation, and the British peregrine is no longer facing extinction; but its status is still delicately balanced, and little would be needed to tip it on a downward path again.

Richard Fyfe

The Peregrine in N. America

To many North Americans the peregrine falcon has become the symbol of man's irresponsibility towards the environment. In the United States initial awareness of the decline of the species, and the resulting stimulus for peregrine field research, came about as a direct result of the 'Peregrine Symposium' held in Madison, Wisconsin in 1965. During this conference the data presented clearly indicated that populations of the peregrine had declined markedly in several European countries as well as in the eastern United States and Canada. At the same time limited documentation of the North American arctic and west coast peregrines suggested that other than on Langara Island in the late 1950s, no declines had occurred in the populations of these two races. During the symposium it was recognized, however, that several factors influenced bird of prey populations, because no single factor, or group of factors, satisfactorily explained the simultaneous and widespread decline of this one species on two continents. It was therefore believed that other unknown factors must be acting on the species. This hypothesis was strengthened by striking similarities in the population declines, which included egg loss through breakage or disappearance, and similar patterns of nest site desertion. European data showing the presence of toxic chemical residues in the eggs and tissues of raptorial birds, and the apparent correlation of population declines of several species with specific agricultural practices in Great Britain, suggested that the organochlorine pesticides or other toxic chemicals might be implicated.

Canadian research worker banding a young peregrine falcon at Bathurst Inlet in the North-West Territories, part of the continuing research program on birds of prey.

In 1966, the pesticide section of the Canadian Wildlife Service initiated a sampling and analysis program on birds of prey.

It was recognized that toxic chemicals would be concentrated in the tissue of birds of prey because of their position at the end of the food chain, and that these species might therefore serve as indicators of residue build-ups in the environment. Since in all probability they would also be the first to reflect detrimental effects of residue build-ups, it was further decided that in addition to samples collected for residue determinations, field research should be undertaken which would include population surveys and certain specific studies. These would be designed to assess the effects of toxic chemical residues and the relative significance of residue build-ups in relation to other factors influencing raptor populations.

Subsequent findings related to mercury and organochlorine contamination of the terrestrial ecosystem have indeed shown that raptorial birds are good indicators of residue build-ups in the ecosystem and the resulting data on residue build-ups in birds of prey and their prey species have figured prominently in Canada in more restrictive recommendations and regulations relative to DDT and mercury in 1970 and for organochlorine seed treatments in 1971.

In general terms the results of our initial field surveys indicated declines in arctic and western Canadian peregrine falcon, prairie falcon, Richardson's merlin, and ferruginous hawk populations. Subsequent field studies were oriented not so much towards substantiating the ill effects of toxic chemical residues but to assessing the relative significance of the many factors affecting the populations of these birds. Results suggest that the major factors currently influencing raptor populations in western Canada are: toxic chemical residues through direct poisoning, embryo mortality, and eggshell thinning; changes in land-use patterns eliminating or altering prey species populations; availability of suitable nesting habitat; direct human interference; predation; with the relative significance varying from area to area with the specific diet of each species.

In 1970 the Canadian Wildlife Service joined with observers in the United States in a co-operative survey of peregrine falcon populations. South of 60° N the survey consisted of checking all previously recorded sites together with extensive exploratory surveys in areas of suitable habitat from the Rocky Mountains east to the Atlantic coast.

The results of the 1970 North American Peregrine Survey clearly indicate that at the present time the eastern race of the peregrine falcon is seriously endangered throughout its range. In Canada, only one successful pair of this race was located in the area south of 60° N and east of the Rockies, including the Maritimes and southern Quebec. Two additional pairs which may represent intergrades with the arctic peregrine were found in coastal Labrador. The survey suggests further that the population of the arctic race has declined in both the eastern and western arctic.

In Canada recent data on the status of the west coast peregrine resulting from the provincial surveys are yet to be published; but the present stability of the Langara and Aleutian populations, together with available productivity data, suggest that any initial trend has at least temporarily been stemmed and that this subspecies is not yet seriously endangered. It should be noted that residue determinations of eggs and tissue samples of this race indicate that the birds are carrying substantial organochlorine and mercury residues, suggesting a need for continued monitoring of this population.

Since 1966 the most significant development in raptor conservation, aside from the necessary monitoring of toxic chemical residues and populations, has undoubtedly been the establishment of captive breeding projects both privately and institutionally. Two major institutional projects have started—the first in 1970 by the Canadian Wildlife Service (an agency of the Canadian Government) and the second established in 1971 at Cornell University.

Moderate success has been realized in breeding and raising both peregrines and prairie falcons in captivity, but before the birds can be raised in sufficient numbers for release many problems remain to be researched and techniques perfected. Some of these problems include such aspects as incubation, housing and food requirements, release techniques, and the determination of information necessary for breeding in the different subspecies. One of the more promising techniques currently being investigated is the use of artificial insemination with both imprinted and non-imprinted birds. To date this method has been successful in producing fertile eggs with goshawks, golden eagles, red-tailed hawks, and peregrines.

Without doubt the decline of the peregrine has been the prime motivation for the establishment of the breeding projects, although the purpose of the projects varies from maintaining and breeding the species for future reintroduction, raising the birds for toxic chemical research, or simply as a means of providing birds for the sport of falconry.

Despite differences in motivation, the most striking aspect has been the spirit of co-operation between participating researchers, falconers, and interested public. This has resulted in a free flow of information which is to a large extent co-ordinated and disseminated by the Raptor Research Foundation centered in South Dakota.

Although raptor population trends are not yet satisfactory, the overall picture is generally encouraging, as indicated by the increased interest, research, and co-operation shown by those working towards methods of preserving the peregrine and other birds of prey. Of equal or greater importance is the trend in North America to move away from the persistent toxic chemicals . . . which gives promise of an environment which will again sustain these valuable birds.

Cameron Kepler

West Indian Parrots

The recent history of the West Indian parrots makes sad reading. Since the arrival of Europeans, the parrot family has suffered severe losses—and continues to do so to this day. When Columbus discovered them in 1492, the West Indies harbored an exceptionally large and diverse parrot fauna, well distributed on the wet islands of high elevation. There may have been as many as eight species of large, gaudy macaws; in addition, there were eleven species of large parrot in the genus *Amazona*, and four species of parakeet.

With European settlement, at least twenty-one species and subspecies of birds became extinct, and no less than thirteen of these were members of the parrot family, including all the macaws and two amazon parrots. Of the remaining nine amazons, five are now threatened with extinction. The parakeets have suffered less, but an endemic Guadeloupe species and a unique race of the Hispaniolan parrot from Mona Island (halfway between Puerto Rica and Hispaniola) have been exterminated.

From 1968 through 1971 I studied the Puerto Rican parrot as a field biologist with the US Department of the Interior's Endangered Wildlife Research Program; my study was also supported by the World Wildlife Fund and the US Forest Service. During this period I visited nearly all the West Indian islands where amazon parrots occur. Many of the factors that formerly reduced the Puerto Rican parrot to very low numbers still apply throughout the West Indies, and so consideration of this species provides an insight into the kinds of problems currently faced by the others.

Historically, the Puerto Rican parrot ranged throughout Puerto Rico, and a distinctive race, now extinct, was found on nearby Culebra Island. The species was known to have occurred in large flocks in 1836, and it continued to be relatively common until the late nineteenth century, although a reliable report in 1878 mentioned that it abounded 'principally in the island's interior', suggesting that lowland populations were becoming scarce. During an intensive study of Puerto Rican birds in 1911 and 1912, Dr Alexander Wetmore found that parrots were nearly exterminated from the western two-thirds of the island, with only a few small flocks remaining in some rugged mountainous sections. They were still relatively common in and around the Luquillo Mountains in eastern Puerto Rico, at that time the least populous and most inaccessible part of the island. In 1931 another naturalist wrote that parrots had completely disappeared from western Puerto Rico, and in the east were found only on the higher slopes of the mountains. Thus within the span of a lifetime the birds had decreased from island-wide flocks of thousands to a mere handful on a single forested mountain. I have talked with elderly Puerto Ricans who can remember, years ago, staying home from school to scare flocks of parrots from their parents' corn fields.

This period of steep parrot decline—1836 to 1931— was a period of rapid human population increase on the island. During the nineteenth century the population climbed from 155,000 (1800) to nearly 1,000,000 (1900), and by 1920 there were approximately 1,300,000 people. The greatest deforestation in the island's history occurred at this time, and ultimately over 99 per cent of the forests were felled or severely altered. Puerto Rican parrots are absolutely dependent upon mature forests for food— and, equally important, nest sites, for they only nest in cavities in trees. There was thus less and less habitat for them. They were hunted for sport in the diminishing forests, and their nests were robbed and the young taken for pets. When they left the forests to seek food in agricultural lands, they were shot, presumably in great numbers. Introduced predators, primarily rats, now prey upon eggs and young, and must have done so in the past as well.

It is quite clear that the greatest parrot decline was due entirely to the activities of man. What has happened to the remaining parrot flock in its isolated stronghold? Over 28,000 acres of the Luquillo Mountains are protected as the Luquillo Experimental Forest, under the administration of the US Forest Service. The upper slopes of this reserve consist predominantly of virgin forest—the largest single virgin tract in the island. The surrounding lands have always been sparsely settled compared to the rest of Puerto Rico (1949 figures: 120 people per square mile, compared with 647 per square mile island-wide), and the areas presently occupied by parrots have never been inhabited. Hunting has been completely prohibited within the forest, and deforestation has been halted, although some large trees have been removed. Thirty years ago one would have predicted that the occurrence of the last parrots within this 40-square-mile forest reserve would protect the species in perpetuity. Unfortunately, this has not been the case.

From 1953 to 1956 surveys of the parrot flocks were made, and the population was reliably estimated at 200 birds. By 1966, however, there were about 50 birds, and when I arrived in late 1968, less than 30. The largest flocks seen in that and subsequent years consisted of 19, 18, 16, and 12 birds respectively, a 94 per cent decline from 1954, and a current annual decrease of 12 per cent. Other measures of parrot numbers indicate a slightly steeper decline. The estimated total wild population in 1971 was less than 15 birds.

The reasons for such a decline within a protected reserve are many: nests are subject to heavy predation— two nests were found in 1971, and both were destroyed by predators. In the last three breeding seasons, 1969 to 1971, four out of five known nests have been unsuccessful. Introduced rats (*Rattus rattus*), and a native bird, the pearly-eyed thrasher (*Margarops fuscatus*), whose population has recently expanded, are largely responsible for these losses. One possible serious blow to the parrots was a result of the Second World War. Puerto Rico was faced with a fuel shortage during the war, and as a result the Forest Service allowed a limited charcoal-making pro-

Though the Hispaniolan parrot is still widespread on Dominica, it is diminishing as the forests are cleared.

gram within the forest boundaries. Unfortunately old Colorado trees (*Cyrilla racemiflora*) were selectively removed. We have since learned that Puerto Rican parrots in Luquillo nest in no other kind of tree! Thus an unknown number of nest sites were lost. (This is only one of hundreds of dramatic examples of the inter-relationships between living things that can be cited, and shows the decisive need for sound research on species that are threatened.) In an attempt to create new nest sites, we provided known nesting areas with nest boxes, but the parrots did not use them.

A more important cause of the parrot decline involves the inherent nature of the rainforest. The wettest area in Puerto Rico, it receives 200 inches of rain in an average year. At higher elevations more rain falls, temperatures are lower, winds are stronger, cloud cover is more persistent, trees are shorter, and plant diversity and productivity decrease. Higher up where parrots are most common there are fewer than half the bird species found at lower elevations, and those that do occur, tend to be less abundant. The higher zones appear to lack some essential factor or factors that the parrots need, even though they are the best remaining forests in Puerto Rico. The lower number of bird species at higher elevations and the gradual decline in the parrot suggest this. In addition, another Puerto Rican bird, the white-necked crow (*Corvus leucognaphalus*), formerly widespread on the island, suffered a decline in range similar to that of the parrot, and was ultimately restricted to Luquillo Forest. Large flocks of thirty years ago became fewer, and the last crows were seen in 1963, in areas the parrots now frequent. The Puerto Rican parrots are following an ominously parallel trend, and probably will not survive the present decade as a wild species.

Because the Puerto Rican parrot appears doomed in the wild, we decided to try to breed it in captivity in a last-ditch effort to save it from extinction. Hopefully a large captive flock can be built up, and some birds released into more suitable habitat in Puerto Rico. A specially-designed aviary has been built at the Patuxent Wildlife Research Center in Maryland, and Hispaniolan parrots, still relatively common in the Dominican Republic, were sent to Patuxent in 1970 for preliminary research in avicultural techniques on the West Indian amazons. Two Puerto Rican parrots, the world's only known captive birds, were transferred from a small Puerto Rican zoo to Patuxent in 1971, and a wild parrot from Luquillo was captured and sent there early in 1972. The future of the species clearly rests with these three birds, and any others captured within the next few years.

So it is important to remember that a common and widespread species was brought to the verge of extinction in less than a hundred years, due mainly to the combined effects of habitat destruction and hunting, and that a rather large (forty square miles) forest reserve proved inadequate, because of its peculiar ecological characteristics, as a preserve for the isolated small popu-

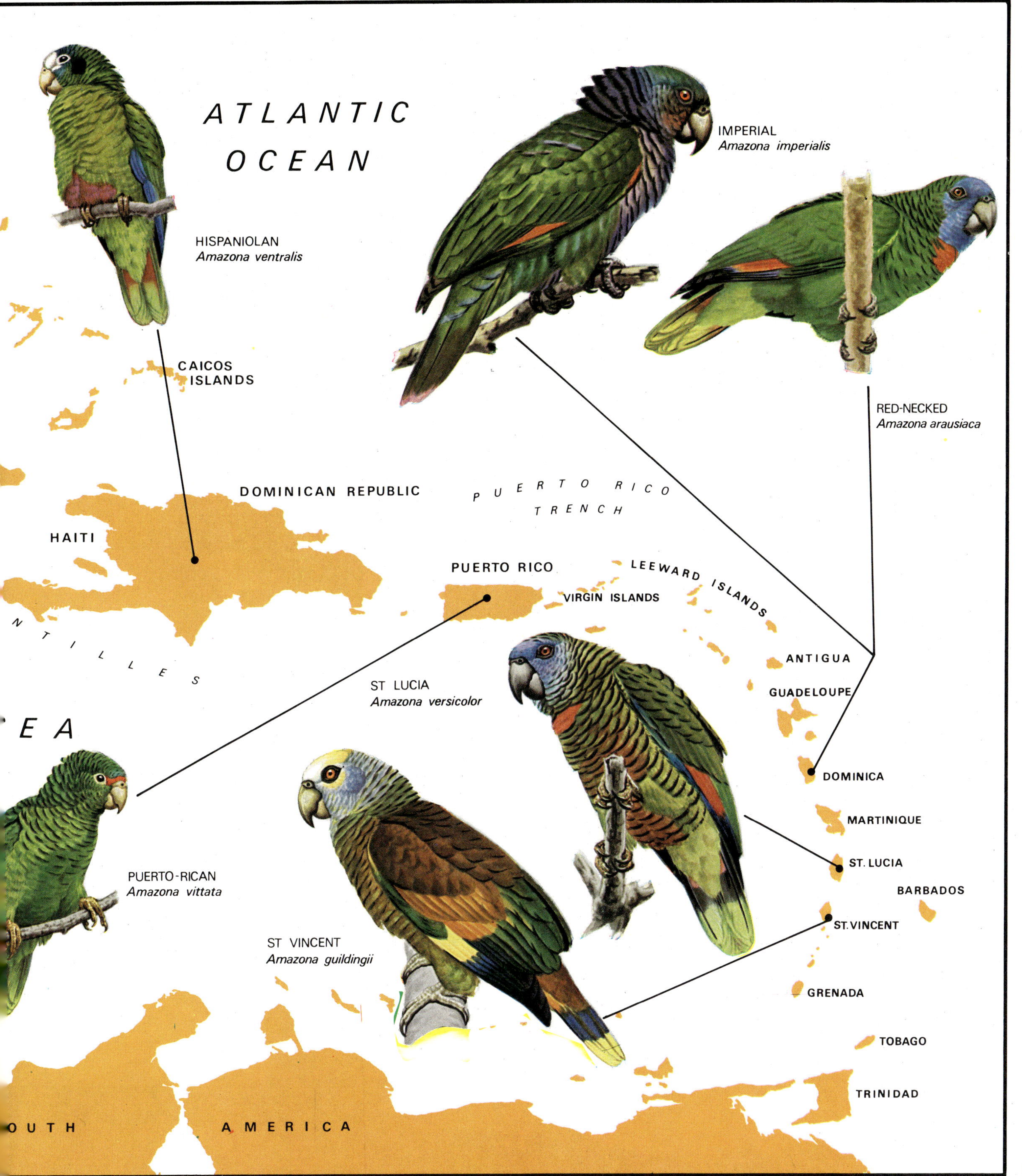

ATLANTIC
OCEAN
HISPANIOLAN
Amazona ventralis
IMPERIAL
Amazona imperialis
RED-NECKED
Amazona arausiaca
CAICOS
ISLANDS
DOMINICAN REPUBLIC
HAITI
PUERTO RICO
TRENCH
N T I L L E S
PUERTO RICO
VIRGIN ISLANDS
LEEWARD ISLANDS
ANTIGUA
GUADELOUPE
ST LUCIA
Amazona versicolor
E A
PUERTO-RICAN
Amazona vittata
DOMINICA
MARTINIQUE
ST. LUCIA
BARBADOS
ST VINCENT
Amazona guildingii
ST. VINCENT
GRENADA
TOBAGO
TRINIDAD
OUTH   AMERICA

THE PAST AND PRESENT DISTRIBUTION AND STATUS OF WEST INDIAN PARROTS

Island	Macaw	Parrot	Parakeet
Cuba	★Cuban red macaw *Ara tricolor*	Cuban parrot *Amazona leucocephala* ☆Races on Grand Cayman, Little Cayman, Cayman Brac, Bahamas	Cuban parakeet *Aratinga euops*
Jamaica	★Jamaican red macaw *Ara gossei* ★Jamaican green & yellow macaw *Ara erythrocephala*	Yellow-billed parrot *Amazona collaria* ☆Black-billed parrot *Amazona agilis*	Olive-throated parakeet *Aratinga nana*
Hispaniola		Hispaniolan parrot *Amazona ventralis*	Hispaniolan parakeet *Aratinga chloroptera* ★Race on Mona Island
Puerto Rico		☆Puerto Rican parrot *Amazona vittata* ★Race on Culebra	
Guadeloupe	★Guadeloupe red macaw *Ara guadeloupensis* ★Guadeloupe violet macaw *Ara purpurascens*	★Guadeloupe parrot *Amazona violacea*	★Guadeloupe parakeet *Aratinga labati*
Dominica	★Dominica green & yellow macaw *Ara atwoodi*	☆Imperial parrot *Amazona imperialis* ☆Red-necked parrot *Amazona arausiaca*	
Martinique	★Martinique macaw *Ara martinica*	★Martinique parrot *Amazona martinica*	
St Lucia		☆St Lucia parrot *Amazona versicolor*	
St Vincent		☆St Vincent parrot *Amazona guildingii*	
?	★Mysterious macaw *Ara erythrura*		

KEY

★—Extinct

☆—In considerable danger of extinction

lation. No one in 1836, or in 1878, would have predicted such a rapid and inevitable decline. This must be borne in mind as we consider parrots elsewhere in the West Indies.

Eight other amazon parrots survive in the West Indies, four in the Greater Antilles, and four in the Lesser Antilles. The Greater Antillean species are much more numerous and widespread on their respective islands than the others. Very little is known about the Cuban parrot. I am told that the Cayman Island races are threatened as land is being rapidly cleared by land speculators, and the Bahama race, now restricted to a single island, is listed as rare and endangered by the International Union for Conservation of Nature and Natural Resources (IUCN). Two species inhabit Jamaica. The yellow-billed parrot is the more widespread, occurring in little-frequented forested regions in the 'cockpit' (limestone karst) country of the north-west, and in even wilder and more remote wet forests on the John Crow Mountains. The black-billed parrot is restricted to localized areas in the cockpit country, and is not a common bird.

In the Dominican Republic the Hispaniolan parrot is widespread and abundant in high mountain forests, but is everywhere retreating as the land is converted to agricultural use. There is no adequate protection for any parrot on these islands, and they are avidly hunted and young are collected for pets. At the same time, their forest reserves continue to shrink, and in many places consist of isolated patches. In visiting these countries one is very much reminded of the early descriptions of Puerto Rico. Indeed, we saw 250 parrots flying from forests in the Dominican Republic to Haitian croplands, and back, on each of five days in a border area—and the spectacle closely matched stories we have heard of Puerto Rican birds years ago. On these islands most birds are hunted, even tiny ones, and there is no inviolate preserve to which parrots can retreat. Human populations are mushrooming as never before. Although these parrots are not now rare, they will certainly become so as present trends continue.

The situation in the Lesser Antilles is more desperate, and simultaneously more hopeful. Three of the four amazon parrots are listed as rare and endangered by the IUCN. However, the governments of the three islands concerned—St Vincent, St Lucia, and Dominica—have legislation protecting the birds, and on St Vincent there appears to be quite widespread awareness of the uniqueness of their endemic parrot—it is portrayed on their postage stamps, for instance, and on maps of the island. It is illegal to hunt the birds, and we did see a pair in lowland agricultural areas. However, some birds are still shot each year, usually in the hopes of obtaining live birds for the pet trade. When we visited St Vincent in 1971 we were told of one such hunter who killed 'about twenty' parrots in the Buccamet Valley, one of the few parrot areas. We saw seven parrots in Hermitage Valley, but these birds were flying over primary forest next to a logging operation that is driving them farther and farther into the mountain forests, which only stretch about eight miles along the center of the island. As this small amount of suitable parrot habitat disappears, parrot numbers have to diminish as a result. No amount of protective legislation will help the species if preferred habitats are not identified and preserved immediately, and all hunting forcefully stopped.

A similar situation exists in St Lucia. Deforestation for banana plantations has completely destroyed huge forest areas in the last thirty years, especially around Piton Flore and south along the Barre de l'Isle Ridge, and parrots are now essentially restricted to about twenty-five square miles of good forest around Mt Gimie. This is a protected reserve, and if present plans to establish an inviolate reserve in the area are carried out, the St Lucia parrot should survive. The bird is legally protected, but is still hunted, and wardens to this day lack power to search a hunter's bag. Thus parrots can be taken with impunity. An expansion of the warden's powers is needed. Some forested parts of the reserve are also being managed for timber, and native trees are being replaced by fast-growing trees, especially blue mahoe. Parrots cannot use these exotic forests, so this is an added threat to them. Only if the present reserve is completely protected, and all hunting stopped, can the St Lucia parrot be expected to survive.

The remaining island, Dominica, has two species of parrots and considerable acreage, for its size, of undisturbed forest, much of it in forest preserves. The most important area for the imperial parrot, a magnificent 18- to 20-inch-long bird, is centered about the higher slopes of Morne Diablotin. It lives in wild areas, but is by no means a common bird—we failed to see it in three days on Morne Diablotin, and were assured by local residents of its scarcity. We were very surprised (and concerned) to hear that hunting parties from nearby Guadeloupe and Martinique make special trips to Morne Diablotin just to hunt the imperial parrot, and if this continues, the bird is certainly doomed. The lesson from Guadeloupe bears repeating here. That island has the largest and some of the best remaining rainforest in the Lesser Antilles, but has lost more parrots than any other island in the West Indies. The reasons became obvious to me when I camped in the splendid rainforest at several locations in Guadeloupe—gunshots were constantly heard, even in a National Park. The forests are literally alive with hunters, and small birds, even those common elsewhere, were rare, wary, and hard to find. I have been told that the same is true in Martinique. For large birds like amazon parrots, big forest reserves are not enough—overhunting can, and has, exterminated them. Lacking parrots on their own islands, gunmen now travel to nearby Dominica, and it is possible that they will repeat the same tragic tale in the forests there. All hunting must be stopped if the imperial parrot is to survive. The red-necked parrot, Dominica's second species, is not abundant, and is in danger from land clearing for bananas, and also from logging. In six days of active searching for this species, we saw only four birds, and it should be included in the IUCN's *Red Data Book*.

In summary, no parrot in the West Indies can be considered safe. The Greater Antillean species have no formal protection, and their present state of relative abundance is unlikely to last as their forest reserves shrink. The Lesser Antillean species, although legally protected, are threatened by lack of enforcement of existing laws, hunting pressures, and loss of habitat. Throughout the Caribbean, the apparent near-impossibility of educating impoverished rural populations (whose resources are dwindling as their numbers, and whose demands upon the land double every twenty to thirty years) throws a bleak pall over hopes for the survival of most of these fine birds.

Malcolm Penny

The Birds of the Seychelles

Birds that live on oceanic islands are of great importance, because they may well provide the key to understanding the needs of other species on the continental land masses. Mainland nature reserves are often no more than 'inland islands', surrounded by a sea of man and his works, and the more we know about isolated populations in general, the better will we be able to conserve the birds that live in them. And the best place to study isolated populations is in their remote island homes. This is one good reason for conserving island birds: it is, of course, equally important to conserve these interesting and often beautiful species for their own sakes.

The birds of the Seychelles are fairly well known now, although they have been studied for hardly more than a century. (There are a few islands among the ninety-two which make up the Seychelles and the British Indian Ocean Territory which have never been properly studied, and doubtless there is much more to be learned about the populations of seabirds which live there, but I shall concentrate on the land birds of the central or granitic group of islands.) Several of the land birds are in the *Red Data Book* of endangered species of the International Union for Conservation of Nature, but this rather exaggerates their rarity. Take the brush warbler, for example, which survives now only on the island of Cousin: the total world population can never exceed the carrying capacity of the island, which is probably about one hundred pairs at most. Thus the brush warbler will always be among the rarest birds in the world, but hopefully it will never again be among those threatened with extinction, since the International Council for Bird Preservation acquired the island and declared it a sanctuary. There is always the danger of a devastating fire which could wipe

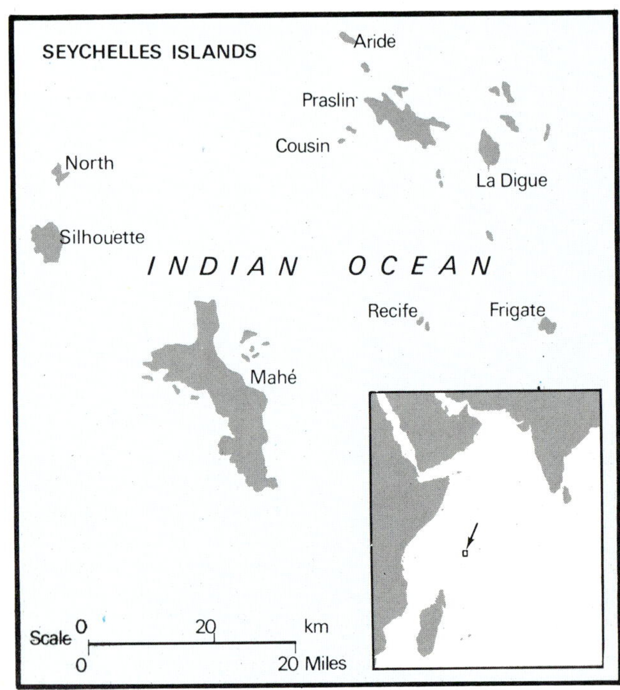

The white-tailed tropic bird nests on the ground, but is safe on rat-free Cousin Island.

out the world population of the warbler at a stroke, but the most careful precautions are taken against that ever happening.

The outstanding Seychelles bird species are not spectacular—island birds seldom are, since they share a common tendency towards drabness of color—but they are of great interest because they live in such a remote place. Questions of how they got there, and why they have evolved as they have, are those which excite ornithologists. Basically the birds of the Seychelles are of mixed African and Madagascan (Malagasy) stock, with only one Asian species, the Chinese bittern, which reaches its westernmost limit in the islands. The rest seem to have come up from Madagascar and the Mascarene Islands—though in the distant past, when the Seychelles was larger than it is now, there may have been some traffic in the opposite direction.

One of the scarcest of the Seychelles birds is the magpie robin, which now survives only on Frigate Island. It is a ground-feeding member of a genus which is much more common in the East than in the West, though it has relatives in Madagascar. Unlike its relatives, however, it is not small, or brightly colored: on the contrary, it is large, the size of an American robin or an English thrush, and black all over save for a white wing-flash. Large size and dark color are both typical of island birds. The *Pie*, as it is known locally, is tame and confiding, omnivorous, and very curious. An early collector who visited Frigate remarked that his men were able to knock the birds down with sticks to collect them for skins. At one time the species was found on Mahé, the main island, as well as on Praslin and La Digue, Marianne and Félicité; but the arrival of man with his retinue of cats and rats soon caused its extinction on all the other islands. Even on Frigate it was reduced to a dangerously low level by feral cats. In 1965 I was with an expedition which counted between twelve and twenty birds on the whole of Frigate. Since then there has been a concentrated drive against cats on the island—so much so that the cats are now nearly extinct, and the population of the *Pie* has increased to about 40 birds, and is still rising. Frigate, being rather isolated from the rest of the Seychelles, also has the densest population of the lovely Seychelles blue pigeon, because the introduced barn owl has not so far reached the island to destroy this bird as it has done elsewhere.

Another very rare species is the black paradise flycatcher of La Digue, which *is* spectacular, the male having a deep blue-black sheen and long flexible tail-streamers. This species, too, was once on Praslin, but because it depends on the lowland tree *Terminalia catappa*, the clearing of the lowland woods led to its probable extinction on that island. Reports have come in recently that there may be one or two pairs on Praslin, but they are unconfirmed, and I would think unlikely. On La Digue, as well, the species is threatened, not only by the felling of the woods, which has not been so extensive there, but

Fairy terns are present in huge numbers on Cousin Island, the first island bird sanctuary in the Indian Ocean. They will lay their eggs in apparently most unsuitable places. This adult bird raised its young actually on the narrow top of the sign board.

The Seychelles magpie robin must be one of the rarest birds in the world, for it is confined to the island of Frigate where it numbers about forty. It used to live on some other Seychelles islands, but man with his retinue of cats and rats caused its extinction on all the others; a drive against feral cats on Frigate Island has caused the population of magpie robins to rise from a low of about fifteen birds to its current level.

by the activities of man—or perhaps one should say, boy. Those magnificent tail feathers seem to be a temptation difficult to resist, and the nest, conspicuous at the end of a dangling twig, makes a challenging target for a slingshot. The Government has acted here to protect the bird: not only are slingshots now illegal on La Digue, but there is a full-time warden whose sole job is to keep an eye on the birds, their nests, and their persecutors. Already there are signs that the population is increasing. This increase is likely to be slow, however, for another characteristic of island birds is that they tend to have a small clutch-size—in the case of the flycatcher one egg, and only very rarely two. The female is quite differently colored from the male, being chestnut and white with a black head, which leads to interesting questions of evolution, for there is another flycatcher far away in New Guinea, supposedly not closely related, in which the

*Confined to the island of La Digue, the black paradise flycatcher (**male left and female right**) is another of the Seychelles' unique bird species. It has a tendency to build its nest on the end of branches suspended over paths in the most populated part of the island. But there is now a full-time warden to keep an eye on the nests, and the flycatcher's numbers are rising.*

division of color between the sexes is exactly the same.

Praslin has its own unique bird, the black parrot, which is now restricted to the few remaining areas of palm forest, notably the nature reserve in the Vallée de Mai, where the unique coco-de-mer palm has its stronghold. At one time the parrot was very common in the fruit-gardens of Praslin, for there are accounts of growers shooting flocks of thirty or more out of their mango trees; but now six or seven at a time is the most that one could hope to see. It is not certain whether the parrot ever existed on Mahé—early accounts of the birds were written by navigators not ornithologists, and they are contradictory on this point—but there was a green parakeet there at one time (now extinct), along with the islands' two species of white-eyes.

In the remaining high forests of Mahé, now strictly protected by law, several interesting birds survive. Two in particular, the bare-legged scops owl and the gray white-eye, had been thought to be extinct until they were rediscovered in the 1960s. The owl is regularly heard, if seldom seen, and its numbers might in fact be considerable; but the white-eye seems to have been reduced to two small flocks in separate areas of the island.

The Seychelles bulbul and the sunbird are two native birds which seem to have suffered little if at all from the activities of man. Both are highly adaptable, and both have learned to feed on introduced animals and plants which their ancestors had never dreamed of. The bulbul has receded a little from the lowlands under pressure from the introduced mynah, but the sunbird nests happily all over the islands, especially on Praslin, where it is among the most common birds.

The same is sadly not true of the Seychelles kestrel, a tiny and beautiful bird of prey which has been ousted from its traditional breeding places in rocks, and latterly in church towers, by the introduced barn owl. In 1950 the Government thought that to introduce a continental predator would help to control rats, without considering what the effect would be on the native endemic birds. As a result the fairy tern is now practically extinct on Mahé and Praslin, and the blue pigeon is going the same way. But there has been some conservation progress here as well: protected by law when it was first introduced, the barn owl now carries a price on its head of thirty rupees ($5.60 or £2.25)—but the damage has been done. The kestrel, meanwhile, has shifted its breeding preference to the open roofs of houses and many residents are proud to have a pair nesting above them. Superstitions about the kestrel remain among the older people—that it is a bird of ill omen, to be killed on sight— but these are dying out in the general wave of conservation awareness that is sweeping the islands.

The showplace of Seychelles ornithology is Cousin Island, the sanctuary owned and managed by the International Council for Bird Protection. Not only is it the last home of the Seychelles brush warbler, a drab bird but a lovely songster, but it has the strongest-established population of the three surviving groups of Seychelles fodies and also the only remnant of the Seychelles race of the turtle dove. There are turtle doves right across the Indian Ocean, all members of the same species, *Streptopelia picturata*, with subspecies on Aldabra, in the Amirantes (probably extinct), and in the Seychelles. However, Indian traders coming to the Seychelles from

NOTABLE LAND BIRDS OF THE SEYCHELLES

Species	Distribution	Whether unique to the Seychelles	Population/trend	Conservation status
Brush warbler *Bebrornis sechellensis*	Cousin only	Unique	85—increasing slowly	Survival seems assured
Chinese bittern *Ixobrychus sinensis*	Mainly on Praslin	No. at westernmost limit of range	?—declining	Protected by law
Magpie robin *Copsychus sechellarum*	Frigate only	Unique	40—increasing	Good protection
Seychelles blue pigeon *Alectroenas pulcherrima*	Mahé, Praslin, Frigate	Unique	?—under pressure from barn owl	Good protection on Frigate
Black paradise flycatcher *Terpsiphone corvina*	La Digue; maybe a few on Praslin Island	Unique	30—increasing	Good protection by full-time warden
Black parrot *Coracopsis nigra barklyi*	Praslin Island only	Unique	50—steady or very slow increase	Protected in Vallée de Mai Nature Reserve
Bare-legged scops owl *Otus insularis*	Mahé only; reports of calls on Praslin	Unique	?—declining	New high forest reserves should help
Gray white-eye *Zosterops modesta*	Mahé only	Unique	?—declining	New high forest reserves should help
Seychelles bulbul *Hypsipetes crassirostris*	All larger islands	Unique	Abundant, except coastal areas of Mahé	Protected by law
Seychelles sunbird *Nectarinia dussumieri*	All islands	Unique	Abundant	Protected by law
Seychelles kestrel *Falco araea*	Mahé, Praslin, ? Marianne	Unique	Uncommon—probably increasing slowly on Mahé; threatened by barn owl, Praslin	Protected by law, but still killed occasionally by superstitious local people
Seychelles fody *Foudia sechellarum*	Cousin, Frigate, Cousine	Unique	500+ Cousin—safe 300 Frigate—steady 250 Cousine—steady	Cousin, fully protected; Frigate & Cousine, protected but subject to loss of habitat
Seychelles turtle dove *Streptopelia picturata*	Pure remnant of Seychelles race only on Cousin	Unique	Declining	Fully protected, but will probably disappear eventually through interbreeding with introduced race

(*Right*) Two fairy terns on Cousin Island. The Seychelles fody (**below left**) lives on three islands. It is protected on all three, and the largest population, on Cousin, can be regarded as safe. One of the most abundant seabirds in the Seychelles is the noddy tern (**below centre**) here at its nest on raised coral. Several Seychelles islands have their unique birds, and the black parrot (**below right**) is Praslin's; it shares the Vallée de Mai nature reserve with another unique and very special species—the coco-de-mer palm.

Mauritius brought with them some doves of Malagasy stock, with the result that the two subspecies have interbred, producing a bird which is neither the one nor the other, but which looks like the Malagasy form. Only on Cousin, for some reason which we do not yet understand, can one find representatives of the pure Seychelles form, with its characteristic reddish head, warm vinous back, and gray underparts.

Cousin is also the home of some of the best seabird colonies in the Seychelles, including the persecuted wedge-tailed shearwater, which has been cropped in the

past as a 'mutton bird', and the smaller and rarer Audubon's or dusky shearwater. White-tailed tropicbirds breed there in huge numbers, safe on the ground of this rat-free island, and the fairy terns and lesser noddy terns are practically impossible to count (though estimates of both species range around 10,000 pairs). Bridled terns, too, find sanctuary on Cousin, along with rare lizards, spiders, and a small coecilian, a legless amphibian like a cross between a frog and a snake.

The island for seabirds, however, is Aride, about ten miles north of Cousin. Here there are colonies of all the seabirds which breed in the Seychelles, though two of them, the red-tailed tropicbird and the greater frigate, may now be extinct as breeding species due to persecution by fishermen in the past. Sooty terns mingle with lesser and common noddies, and wedge-tailed and Audubon's shearwaters; and roseate terns and little terns breed among the rocks where, as on Cousin, fairy and bridled terns are common. The island is up for sale, in case you happen to have about $190,000 (£75,000) or so to spend; but whoever buys it will be firmly restricted in the use he can make of the island, since it is now under the care of the Government.

This control of development is the best thing to have happened in the Seychelles since the first stirrings there of tourist industry, essential if the islands are ever to be anything like economically viable. Now tourism is growing apace, with 100,000 visitors expected in 1975, and gloom has been seen on the faces of naturalists who know and love the islands and their wild places. But the Government of this British colony, in appointing a Nature Conservancy Commission with powers to declare reserves and sites of special interest, has shown that it intends to make sure that the treasures of these lovely islands are protected for all to enjoy. I have hardly mentioned the plant life—the pitcher plants and unique orchids, the six endemic palms, and the incredible 'jellyfish tree'; nor the endemic terrapin and the five species of tree frogs which live in the high moss-forest (how did *they* cross a thousand miles of salty ocean to get there?); nor the two rare and harmless snakes, and the many other unique forms of life, especially the marine life. But you can see it all if you go there.

All this wealth of wildlife is now in the care of the Seychelles Government, who are taking the best available advice in preserving the land and the sea in the face of tourism. It is to be hoped—and confidently—that those 100,000 visitors in 1975, and all their successors, will have plenty to see in the Seychelles. This will not only delight the rarity-hunter, but it will provide scientists with the natural material they need to study if we are to preserve those other, artificial, islands which we are creating in the world we are so rapidly overwhelming.

73

Arturo Osio

New Laws for Italian Birds

Hunters are often the keenest of conservationists, for they are well aware that if they don't conserve today there will be nothing to hunt tomorrow. But this is not so in every country, and in Italy, for instance, hunters and conservationists are locked in almost continuous battle. Hunters, in fact, are one of the most serious threats to wildlife in that country, where about two million armed men, with a territorial density of eighteen hunters per square mile (the highest in the world), fire more than one billion cartridges every year from August through April. They aim their guns at about 150 different creatures, mostly birds—and indeed there used to be no limitation at all on the killing of migratory birds. The hunters are a large and powerful lobby.

One of the few organizations campaigning to bring Italian hunting activity within reasonable limits is the Associazione Italiana per il World Wildlife Fund (the Italian National Appeal of the World Wildlife Fund). Since it was launched in 1966, World Wildlife Italy has spoken out against the hunters' excesses, proposed better game laws, and sought to influence the hunting associations.

Two important achievements have resulted from this campaign. The first of these concerns bird-netting, which has been widely practised for centuries in northern Italy. The story starts with the Italian Parliament passing a new which would have made bird-netting illegal as of 1970. But hardly had the rejoicing by conservationists subsided when the World Wildlife Fund got word of another new law being prepared. The latest legislation would have had the effect of allowing this type of hunting again, but under a different guise. So World Wildlife mounted a last-minute campaign to inform the public about what was being planned, and the disastrous effect it would have on Italy's birdlife.

Help came from all parts of the country, and from abroad as well. Protests were delivered to Members of Parliament, and to top government officials. But all was in vain, and during the first few days of 1970—ironically designated as European Conservation Year—the Italian Parliament approved this cynically drafted legislation. Once more, Italy's birds could be caught in nets.

But although they had suffered a setback, the Italian conservationists refused to be defeated, and sought the help of the country's most important daily paper, *Il Corriere della Sera* of Milan. A committee was formed by World Wildlife Italy and the other Italian conservation and animal welfare groups. Between them, and with the active help of the newspaper, they quickly collected over half a million signatures on a petition against bird-netting.

This remarkable response had one very important result: it made Italian politicians much more sensitive to public opinion when dealing with the problems of hunting. A second result was that it forced the politicians

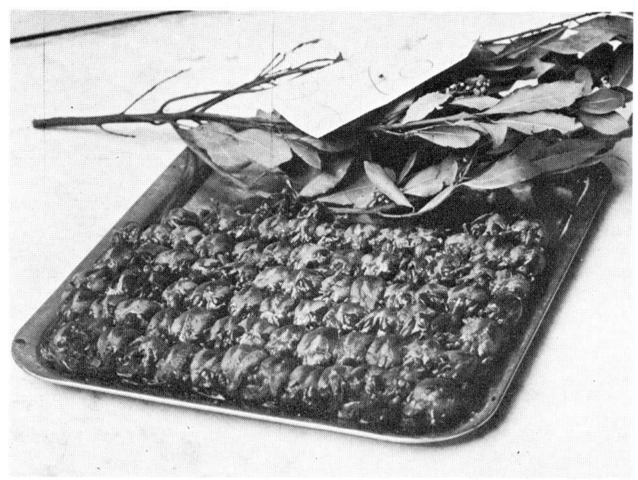

Plucked and ready for cooking—a common sight in Italy.

to greatly limit the application of the new law. And finally, it provoked the Senate into approving yet another new law forbidding once again—and totally, this time—the practise of bird-netting.

Unfortunately, this latest law did not complete all its stages, due to new elections pending, and will have to be submitted again to both branches of Parliament. But at last success seems within our grasp. As I write this, bird-netting is officially prohibited. It is only carried on where certain local authorities, under a special provision, issue limited licenses—which anyway forbid the killing of the captured birds.

The other important achievement concerns the spring hunting of migratory birds. Until 1970 hunting was allowed until mid-May, and the hunters' guns were aimed at the host of birds, especially quail and turtle doves, which reached the Italian coast exhausted after their annual migratory flight from North Africa. Other targets included bee-eaters, cuckoos, hoopoes, various waders, and many birds of prey. The spring hunt was particularly popular in Sicily, Calabria, and Apulia, where it is a long-established tradition. But 1970 was to be the last year, for in 1967 a law had been passed prohibiting spring bird hunting as of 1971.

Despite considerable pressure from hunters and gunsmiths, both at local and national level (including a protest march by some 20,000 hunters through the streets of Rome), the spring hunt did not take place in 1971. But a new threat loomed in 1972 when the Italian Regional Governments were granted autonomy in certain matters—including the administration of hunting laws. Many regions—Apulia, Campania, and Calabria among them—lost no time in introducing local laws to re-allow the ill-famed spring bird hunt. Immediately World Wildlife and other bodies went into action, especially in southern Italy, and mounted a successful counter-attack against the powerful political forces supporting the hunters.

The result was that only a few days after the regional

Italian duck-hunters—a powerful lobby who are likely to continue their fight to get the ill-famed spring hunt reinstated.

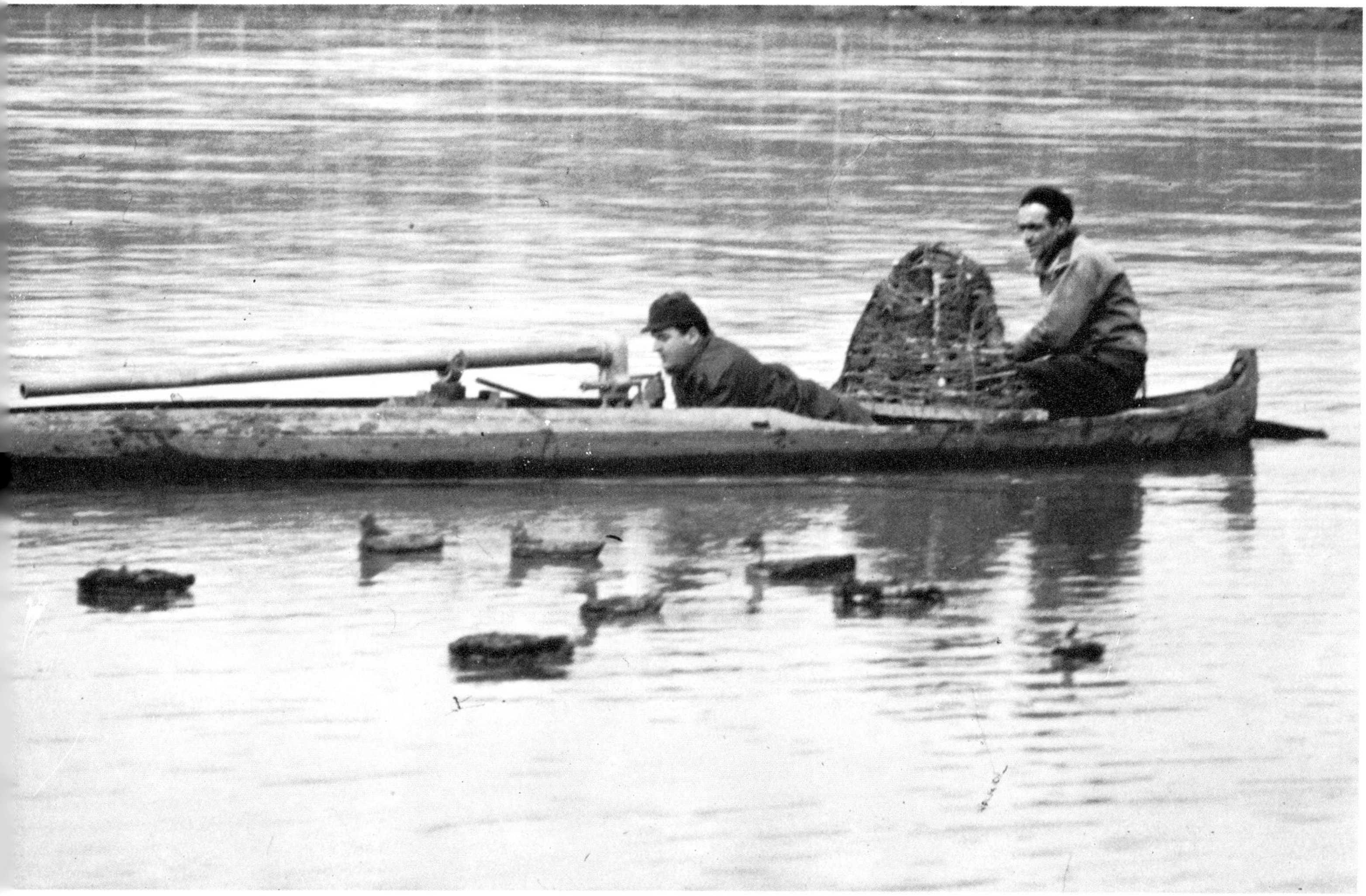

There are eighteen hunters to the square mile in Italy, the highest density in the world, and they aim their guns at almost anything that moves. Until recently there was no limitation at all on the hunting of migratory birds.

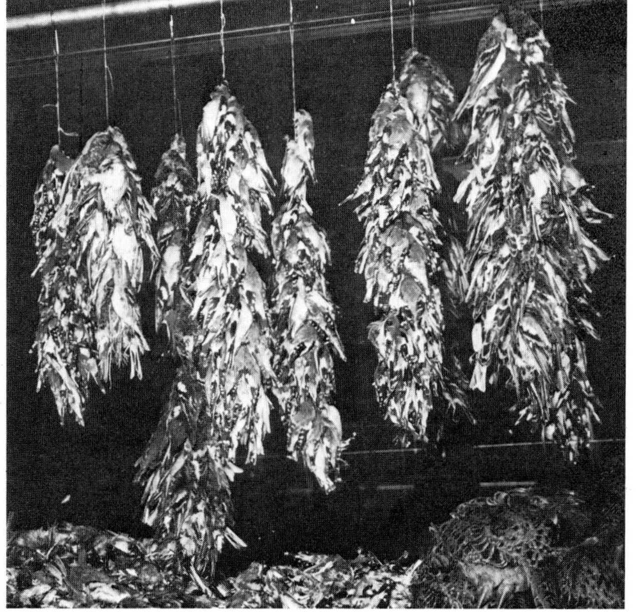

laws had been announced, the central Government in Rome intervened decisively and had them all revoked. Although a few hunters refused to accept the new situation, the hunting season remained officially closed throughout Italy after 31 March 1972. The effects were soon evident. The number of nesting birds increased considerably, and ornithologists were able to report a dramatic increase in the population of raptors such as falcons, kites, buzzards, the short-toed eagle, and the Egyptian vulture.

The fight will certainly continue in the years to come, as the hunters of southern Italy have by no means accepted defeat. But year by year the birds of Italy are getting a better deal. The next major objective of Italian conservationists is the total protection of all birds of prey. So far they have managed only to have them removed from the list of pests, which can be hunted all the year round. But hopes are high that in the near future no one will be allowed to shoot at any bird of prey in Italy, at any time.

Minke whale underwater. The smallest and most recent of the baleen whales to be hunted.

The Great Whales

Commercial Sealing

The Sea Otter Success Story

Nigel Sitwell

The Great Whales

Stop slaughtering whales for ten years! That was the clear message from the world's biggest conservation conference in Stockholm, Sweden, in June 1972. The proposal for a global moratorium on commercial whaling came about halfway through the mammoth conference, and put new spirit into the 1,500 delegates. Many of them were showing signs of fatigue as they faced the daily mountains of paperwork which ny United Nations conference generates. And, too, the Stockholm conference had seemed as if it might fail to rise above basic political prejudices and get to grips with the real environmental and conservation issues.

The whales—perhaps because they were so relatively unpolitical—helped give the conference real meaning. The United States, who had few friends on other Stockholm issues, led the way by proposing the moratorium on whaling. A number of countries unexpectedly voted for conservation (and apparently against their national interests) and spoke in support of the motion. Norway, for instance, still a whaling nation, voted in favour; so did Chile, though Chile's whaling is somewhat minor league. Others stuck to their guns and spoke against the moratorium (Brazil, Spain, Portugal, South Africa, and Japan); the Soviet Union, one of the largest whaling nations, did not attend the conference.

The position of the world's whales at mid-June 1972 was therefore that fifty-three nations had voted to stop all whaling. But they had also voted to achieve this objective through the International Whaling Commission, a 14-nation body that was due to hold its annual meeting just a week later in London. The eyes of the world were on the IWC, as never before, for this was the first real test of the great Stockholm gathering: would any of the hundred-plus recommendations prove to have real meaning in the weeks and months to come?

As if to emphasize this point Maurice Strong, the energetic Canadian Secretary-General of the Stockholm Conference, flew in to London to attend the opening day of the IWC's deliberations—in order to stress the importance of the moratorium demand, and to point out the strength of world opinion on the subject. However, few but the most optimistic really expected the IWC to agree to abandon whaling, and effectively put themselves out of business. And in the event the cynics were proved right. As the IWC chairman, Professor J. L. McHugh of the United States, put it in a remarkable forthright and revealing statement, 'Stockholm was an expression of opinion; here we are in the real world'. The whalers, businessmen, and government officials of 'the real world' failed to understand why whaling should stop—while there were still whales to be caught.

The fact is that though they *are* still around, the number of great whales available for catching in the world's oceans is tremendously reduced from what it once was. While it is true to say that no whale species has actually become extinct in modern times, many species have been grossly over-exploited . . . to the point

where they have had to be given total protection for a number of years.

The blue whale, the largest animal ever known to have existed, can grow to a length of one hundred feet and a weight of about 360,000 pounds (160 English tons). Once upon a time there were several hundred thousand blue whales, but the voracious whaling industry has changed all that. Over the years blue whale numbers have come tumbling down to a mere few thousand— 12,000 to 14,000 is the current best estimate—a pitiful remnant of this animal's former abundance, especially when you consider that they are spread over colossal areas of the Atlantic, Pacific, and Southern Oceans.

The famous right whales (so named because they were originally said to be the right or correct whales to catch) can now be counted in the low thousands, while humpback whales probably number less than 10,000. The California gray whale is in rather better shape. Completely protected since 1946, it now totals about 11,000; this compares with perhaps 20,000 originally, though some experts believe the present population is as high as it ever was. Mexico has taken a particularly strong

SPECIES & DEGREE OF PROTECTION

Blue Whale
Total protection

Fin Whale
Closed areas, closed season & size limits
1972 Quotas:
5,000 Antarctic
650 N. Pacific

Right Whale
Total protection

Sei Whale
Closed areas, closed season, & size limits
1972 Quotas:
5,000 Antarctic
3,000 N. Pacific

Humpback Whale
Total protection

Gray Whale
Total protection

Minke Whale
1972 Quotas:
5,000 Antarctic

Sperm Whale
Size limits
1972 Quotas:
Southern Hemispheres:
8,000 Males 5,000 Females
North Pacific:
6,000 Males 4,000 Females

0 10 20 30 40 50 60 70 80 90 100 110
FEET

Fin whale blowing in the Gulf of California, Mexico. Of the great whales still hunted, the fin is the largest and also the one giving conservationists the most concern. Even though current quotas provide for a slow recovery of the fin whale's numbers, it is felt that there should be a moratorium on hunting this species until its population recovers to a safer level.

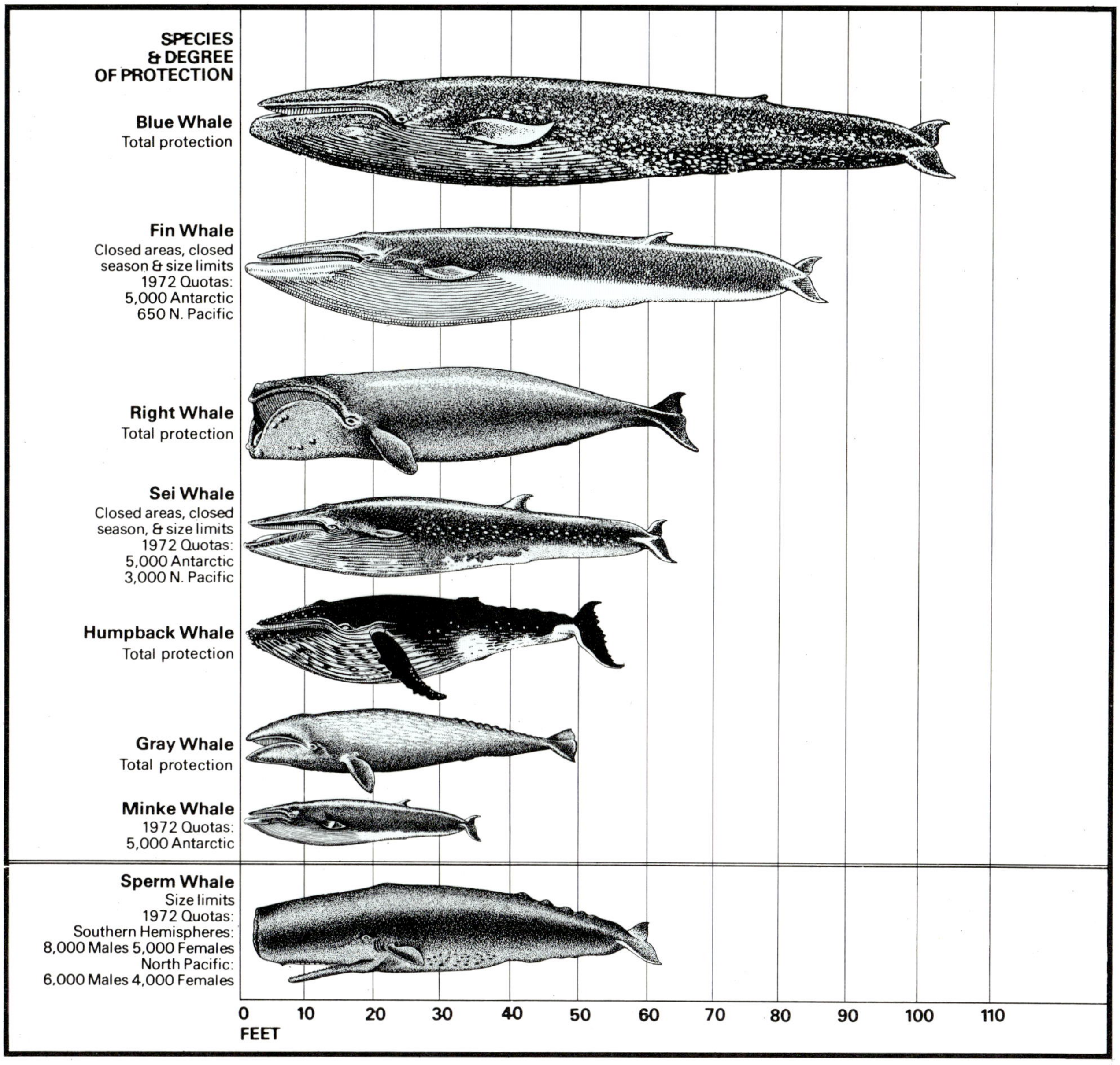

stand in conserving this species, and recently declared Scammons Lagoon, Baja California, a whale refuge—banning all vessels during the calving season.

How have things got to this sorry state? It is hard to comprehend how the industry allowed its raw material (if one can use such a mundane expression to describe such wonderful animals) to be so disastrously over-exploited. The pattern in the past was for the whalers to pursue each species with ruthless zeal until it became uneconomic to seek it out. Then they moved on to the next species down the list. When they had reduced a species virtually to the point of extinction, they called a halt in the name of conservation. The fact that no species have actually become extinct so far is due more to good luck than good management. At this moment in history only three species of great whales still exist in sufficient numbers to be hunted at all—the sei, fin, and sperm whales—and a fourth, Bryde's whale, sometimes included with the sei.

Of these, the fin whale (at about eighty feet the second largest species after the blue) is officially listed as a vulnerable species. Its global population currently stands at about 100,000, or somewhere between a quarter to a fifth of what it once was. And the numbers have still been going down. Sei and sperm whales, however, are in better shape; indeed, some scientists put sperm whale numbers at as much as one million or more.

Faced, then, with an almost unanimous vote of non-confidence in their activities in Stockholm, and a mounting tide of hostile public opinion, what did the whaling

79

men do in London? As I have mentioned, they decided to ignore the call for a complete moratorium. Strictly speaking, such a demand could not be justified on purely scientific grounds. There are undoubtedly enough sei and sperm whales to support a properly regulated annual harvest. But the whaling nations' past performance hardly gave conservationists confidence: all too often in previous years the annual catch limits had been set at levels higher than even their own scientific committee recommended as desirable.

There are other grounds for demanding a moratorium besides the scientific one. Whales are highly intelligent animals, for instance, and the normal method of killing them—with the explosive harpoon—is utterly cruel and barbaric. If it were used on a terrestrial animal it would have been outlawed long ago. All whale products can now be replaced by animal, vegetable, or synthetic substitutes. We no longer use whale oil for lamps, and whalebone, which was widely used for making corset stiffeners amongst other things, has now been replaced by plastic or steel. But whale oil, meat, bone, and other parts of their anatomy do still find their way into fertilizers, canned soups, cosmetics, margarine, soap, and above all, dog and cat food.

*Little is known about the current status of the smaller whale species, though few of them are thought to be in any immediate danger of extinction. However, various small whale species are traditionally hunted in many parts of the world. Here **(above, left, and right)** Faeroe Islanders hunt pilot whales, which can measure up to about twenty-five feet in length. When a school is sighted the animals are herded into shallow water.*

Hunting minke whales with a land-based catching vessel. First the whale is harpooned, then it is hauled out of the water and later pulled aboard the catcher at the stern. It will be taken to a land station in Japan for processing.

The whaling nations decided to go on whaling, but to be fair they did agree various measures to further limit their activities in the years ahead. They agreed, for example, to implement an observer scheme, whereby an observer from one nation will watch over another nation's whaling, to ensure that the IWC's regulations are being followed. This is certainly an important step, though it has been criticized on the grounds that it could be open to abuse. Japan and Russia, for instance, the two nations who dominate the international whaling scene, will exchange observers on their factory ships. Why not have an outsider monitor these operations, one who might be more obviously impartial? But it is perhaps going too far to suggest possible collusion, for the Russians and Japanese are commercial rivals, and of course the Russian fleet is state-owned, while the Japanese is in the hands of private enterprise. Still, stranger things have happened.

The IWC also announced the final disappearance of the old 'Blue Whale Unit'—a system of measuring whale catches without regard to individual species. Thus, one blue whale was equivalent to two fin whales, two and a half humpbacks, or six sei whales. It was a very imprecise conservation tool, for obvious reasons, when used to set quotas. The introduction of the international observer scheme and the abandonment of the BWU were undoubtedly achievements of the 1972 meeting—but hardly a radical advance as the former had been first proposed in 1955, and the latter in 1954!

Besides these measures the fourteen Commissioners set quotas, or catch limits, for the coming season for all of the currently hunted whales. Taking the most endangered species first, a quota for the fin whale was established of 1,950 in the Antarctic and 650 in the North Pacific. This represents a reduction of some 25 per cent on the actual catch in the previous season—but even so, it is not particularly remarkable. If they had decided instead to stop catching fin whales altogether, it would take about twenty-five to thirty years for the stocks to rebuild to a level which would give the 'maximum sustainable yield' (defined as the largest number which can be taken regularly every year without the population declining). And that level is only about half the original number of fin whales in the world. But at the agreed quota level, stocks will of course rebuild much more slowly, taking perhaps fifty years to reach maximum sustainable yield level.

The quotas set for the sei whale (5,000 in the Antarctic and 3,000 in the North Pacific) are thought to be the maximum sustainable yield. For the sperm whale it was decided to allow 13,000 to be caught in the Antarctic and 10,000 in the Pacific—again, an amount considered 'safe' by the whaling scientists. One additional decision was to impose a catch limit for the first time on the small minke whale—5,000 for the Antarctic. This probably is a real achievement, as it is the first time the whalers have set a quota before the exploitation of a particular species has got into high gear.

One of the major failings of the International Whaling Commission is that not every whaling nation is a member. In 1970, for instance, Peru caught nearly 2,000 sperm

Populations of the Great Whales

whales, while Portugal, Spain, Chile, and Brazil accounted for lesser numbers. Yet none of these nations are bound by the IWC regulations. It is vital that all whaling countries should join the IWC, or the limited agreements decided by the IWC will continue to be far less effective than they might be.

A glaring example of why this is so important is that although Japan is herself a member of the IWC, a Japanese company is carrying out whaling operations under the Brazilian flag, out of the port of Recife in the Atlantic. This company is reputed to be catching 1,000 whales annually, and also taking lactating females and possibly calves, both against IWC regulations.

Something else which concerns conservationists—and, to be fair, the IWC as well—is the growing exploitation, intentional or accidental, of a number of the smaller members of the whale family—the dolphins, porpoises, and so on. There is little hard fact to go on so far, but it is reliably estimated that American tuna fishermen kill about 250,000 porpoises every year—by mistake. The trouble is that in certain areas the porpoises associate with the tuna, and the fishermen cannot avoid hauling them in with their catch. However, a research program is being set up in the United States to deal with this problem.

A basic difficulty that faces anyone concerned about whale conservation is access to accurate information. At the moment, much of the basic data is derived from government inspectors on whaling ships—and this situation is unlikely to change, as it would prove extremely costly to mount an independent research operation on whale numbers. Some whale scientists themselves question the validity of population estimates, not because they believe the figures are being fraudulently concocted, but because by the very nature of things there is a built-in bias towards over-estimation. The mathematics are very complex, but in essence the argument is

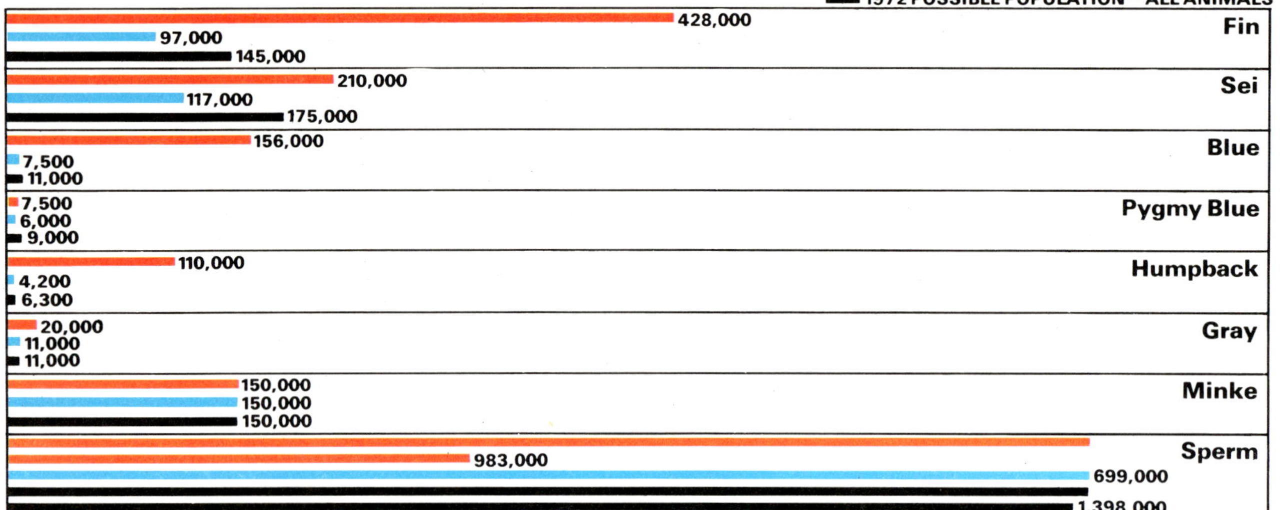

*Many whales and porpoises strand themselves, such as sperm whales **(above left)**, though it is not certain why. One theory is that they become disorientated in unfamiliar territory: The sei whale (seen, **(below left)**, at a whaling station near Durban, South Africa) still exists in fair numbers.*

based on the obvious fact that the whale catchers are going where they think, from their knowledge and experience, that whales will be found. It follows that they are likely to find many more whales than if they were to conduct a random search. So it could be that present estimates of whale populations are too high, and therefore the agreed quotas are themselves too high. In other words, the whaling nations are not being sufficiently prudent.

What of the future? Now that, as expected, the IWC has decided to continue commercial whaling, there is sure to be mounting public pressure around the world. This pressure may take several forms. One action which has been discussed is to boycott Japanese consumer goods in an attempt to persuade the Japanese to give up whaling. It is even suggested that extremist groups might take more violent action, such as blowing up Japanese shipping. Probably more useful is a plan to persuade other nations to join the IWC, and influence its decisions. Whales are, after all, an important global resource, and it should not be the whaling nations alone who decide the fate of the great whales.

Possibly the best way of all to stop commercial whaling would be to remove the market for whale products. The United States has a complete ban on whale products entering the country, under its Endangered Species Act, and in 1972 (during the IWC meeting, in fact) the major British pet food manufacturers announced their decision to stop using whalemeat, thus removing another large slice of the world market.

The most promising augury for the future of the great whales is the strong rumor that Russia is ceasing whaling in a year or two. It appears that she is finding it increasingly uneconomic. In the past it has been difficult for whaling companies to stop because of the large capital investment in their ships: but now the Russians have found an alternative use for the huge factory ships—to use them for catching and processing fish. This may not prove to be so good for the fish, but it is good news for the whales. If the Russians stop, it would be easier to monitor the effects of Japanese whaling on the populations.

So although the moratorium was rejected, 1972 was a year in which the tide began to turn. The future now looks brighter for these huge, intelligent, fascinating animals, brighter than it has looked within living memory.

Colin Platt

Commercial Sealing

Commercial sealing has aroused greater public opposition than any other form of wildlife exploitation—with the possible exception of whaling. Seals, especially the baby whitecoats, are very attractive animals to look at; it takes a hard heart to resist the mute appeal in those big eyes gazing out from the pages of mass circulation newspapers. And it is not surprising that public opinion has been aroused when these charming, furry animals are seen being battered to death with baseball bats, and then slit from one end to the other with a large knife (with the suggestion that some of them may be still alive when the skinning takes place).

But there is a conservation issue, too, which has tended to get overlooked. Recent findings have shown that the harp seal—*Pagophilus groenlandicus*—of the north-west Atlantic has been greatly over-exploited. As a result, sealing operations are being run down in this area. It was predictable, perhaps, that the industry would be exploring new areas in which to carry on its activities—and one potentially lucrative area stands out from all others as being ripe for 'development': Antarctica.

To put this new prospect into perspective, let us look at the annual harvest of harp seals in the north-west Atlantic, and particularly the Gulf of St Lawrence. Each sealing season in recent years has been a growing and unprecedented number of scientists, observers, reporters, photographers, and (regrettably) many sensation-seekers gathering on the Gulf's Magdalen Islands. The outcome has been important new data about the habits of this species. In a way, the Gulf of St Lawrence in the last six years or so has been a testing ground for the rational exploitation of a natural resource. After concentrated observation, research, and negotiation, we are at last seeing the results.

The Greenland, or harp, seal is so named because its brown back markings are thought to be shaped like a harp (although I have examined thousands, I myself cannot see the similarity). It has strong migratory instincts, and spends the summer months from May to October in the seas off southern Greenland. Three distinct groups are recognized, and they do not interbreed; during October they migrate to Labrador, Jan Mayen Island, and the White Sea, respectively, where they spend the winter. The young are born during the first week of March, but during the first month of its life a seal pup is unable to swim—hence the need for sea ice as a breeding ground.

Lactation is short by mammalian standards, lasting only seven to ten days during which the pup increases from a birth weight of about thirty pounds to a weaning weight of about eighty pounds. For the next two weeks after weaning the pup is completely ice-bound, and survives off its body fats until it enters the water for the first time at the age of four to five weeks, where it feeds on crustaceans.

The mother seals abandon their pups about fourteen

Crabeater seals off
the Argentine
Islands, Antarctica.
This is the most
abundant of the six
Antarctic species.

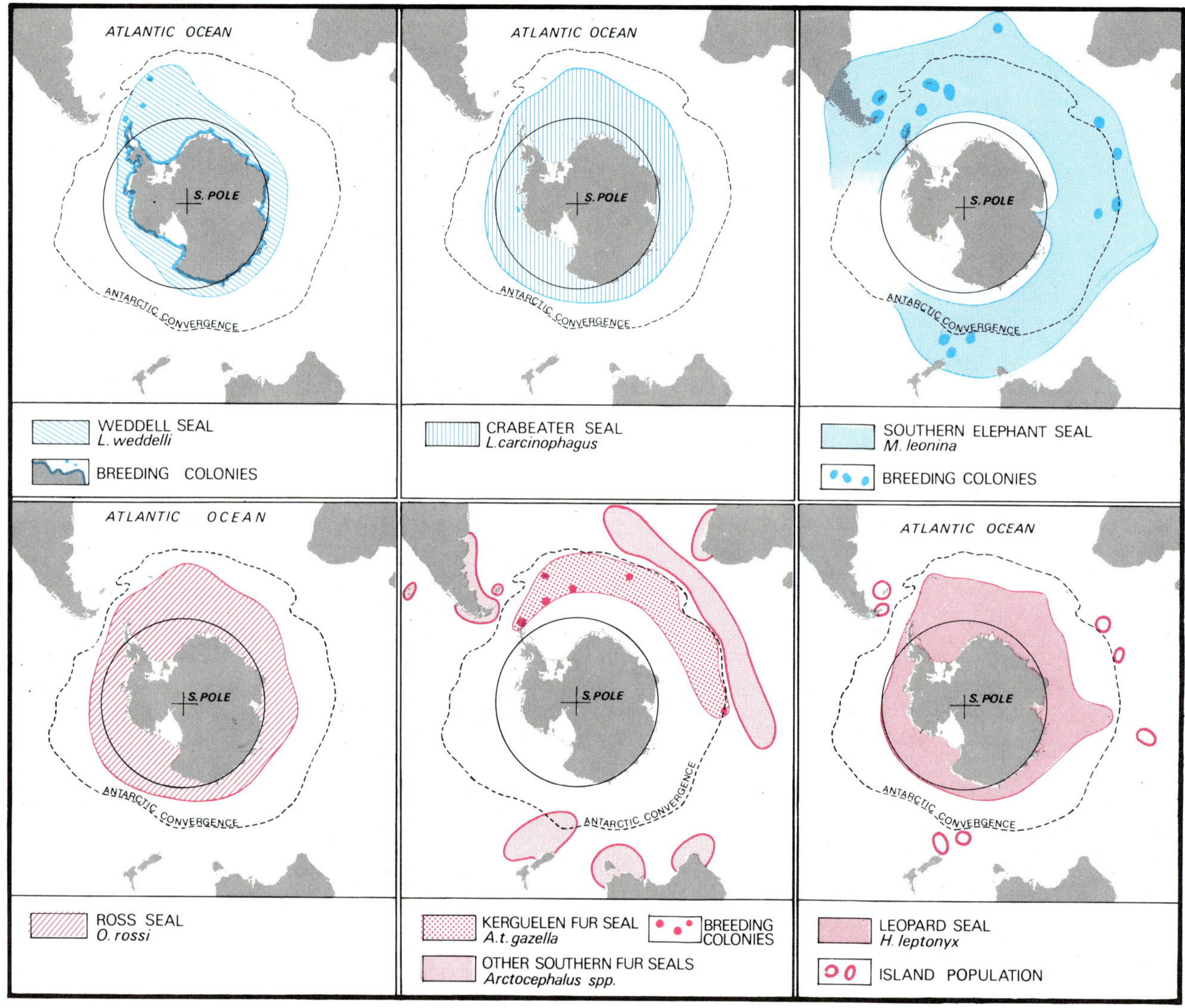

days after birth, and swim to the outer ice limits to feed. They do not rejoin the pups in the breeding colonies but instead join groups of mature and immature seals some-times a hundred miles from the breeding colonies, where molting and mating take place during the ensuing month. Early in May the various groups, or herds, start their migration back to Greenland—being joined on the way by the pups that have survived the attentions of the sealers.

The gestation period of the harp seal is ten months, after a two-month delayed implantation. I have already mentioned that the sea ice is vital for the survival of the pups during the first four weeks of their lives: if im-plantation took place immediately after mating, the pups would be born in January when ice conditions are unsuitable.

Excessive over-exploitation of the harp seal for the last decade has reportedly caused changes in the species' reproductive pattern. One result is earlier puberty. In the Labrador herd, seals now reach puberty at the age of four to six, compared with an age of six to seven some ten years ago. It remains to be seen if this will in turn result in earlier sterility.

Throughout its range the harp seal has been heavily exploited, both by land-based operations and by pelagic expeditions. It is estimated that the harp seal originally numbered about 10 million; of this total, the Labrador herd numbered 5 million animals, the Jan Mayen herd 1 million, and the White Sea herd 4½ million. By the mid-1960s this total had shrunk to an estimated 3 million, and drastic measures were introduced to arrest the rapid decline. Opening and closing dates were established for the annual sealing seasons. Russia imposed a limit of 20,000 on pups taken by landsmen in the White Sea. A Russian-Norwegian agreement limited the size of the vessels operating in the Jan Mayen and Novaya Zemla areas. The Canadians limited the harvest of pups in the Gulf of St Lawrence to 50,000.

But in the north-west Atlantic, off the Labrador and Newfoundland coasts, unrestricted killing continued

Southern elephant seal, photographed at the Valdes Peninsula, Argentina. In the Antarctic, this species will be completely protected under the convention recently agreed by the Antarctic Treaty nations.

from Canadian and Norwegian vessels, and from small boats based on the mainland. The north-west Atlantic ('Front') sub-herd decreased by 60,000 between 1950 and 1960. By 1969 the total number of pups born in both Gulf and Front sub-herds was 300,000, decreasing by 25,000 annually. The number which could safely be harvested each year without affecting the overall population size—the sustainable yield—was 125,000. But the annual pelagic kill was 220,000, and landsmen killed a further 40,000.

The International Commission for North-west Atlantic Fisheries (ICNAF) fixed quotas for the 1971 season at 50,000 and 150,000 for the Gulf and Front respectively. But these quotas, when added to the landsmen's catch, accounted for the whole year's young seal population!

Faced with overwhelming scientific evidence that the present rate of exploitation was endangering the Labrador herd, and in view of mounting public opinion calling for an end to sealing, the Canadian Minister for Fisheries, Jack Davies, established a specialist Committee on Seals and Sealing (COSS) to review all aspects of the problem. COSS presented an interim report to the Minister just before the start of the 1972 season. The contents of the report, which included the most recent population estimates arrived at with the aid of a computer at the University of Guelph, caused the Minister to intervene immediately and cancel all pelagic sealing in the Gulf of St Lawrence.

Canada and Norway are now considering a moratorium on the killing of harp seals in the north-west Atlantic, embodying a planned phase-out by 1975. Significantly, the COSS report recommends that Canada should not allow exploitation of other marine mammals as a substitute for the harp seal—and that this restriction should apply to all waters. This appears to be a direct reference to the suggestion that Canadian sealing interests might make up for the loss of the harp seals by taking crabeaters in the Antarctic. I hope that Canada will accept the COSS recommendation and resist this temptation.

Will the Antarctic be next?

At present there is no commercial sealing going on in the Antarctic, but with the estimated populations of crabeater, Weddell, and leopard seals offering annual sustainable yields of 175,000, 5,000 and 12,000 respectively, it is clear that sooner or later interest is likely to develop. Anticipating this possibility, the twelve Antarctic Treaty nations met in London in 1972 to strengthen the existing arrangements which already give total protection to seals on the Antarctic continent itself—but not on the sea ice. The idea was to prevent a repetition of the over-exploitation which has affected so many marine mammal species—and to do this by establishing in advance detailed and safe annual quotas that would not harm any of the seal populations.

Are we being a little over-pessimistic about the possible scale of sealing operations in the Antarctic? And is it really likely to happen anyway? To take the second point first, I believe it is entirely likely. There are, after all, many similarities between the whaling and sealing industries, and during the 1920s and 1930s pelagic whaling was at its height in the Northern Hemisphere, with dire consequences for the great baleen whales. The whalers then turned their unwelcome attentions to the Antarctic. The possibility is strong of the sealers doing the same, having over-exploited the northern fur seal, the harp, hood, and gray seals in the Bering Sea, the north-west Atlantic, the Arctic, the Barents and White Seas, and round the coasts of northern Europe.

I believe also that concern about the possible level of their activities is fully justified on the industry's past record. There is no evidence to suggest that the sealers would themselves regulate the number of animals taken, or employ a rational policy of herd management, without outside interference. Here are a few examples from the past:

Between 1783 and 1812 the Falkland Islands' population of southern elephant seals was exterminated;

Seventeen sealing vessels visited South Georgia in 1800 and killed 112,000 fur seals. The US sealer *Aspasia*, from New York, alone accounted for 57,000;

Weddell reported in 1823 that over 1,000,000 seals had been taken in South Georgia, and that the herds were effectively destroyed;

Sealers visited the South Shetlands in 1820–21, and in that single year exterminated all 250,000 seals;

During the eighteenth and nineteenth centuries the southern elephant seal was brought to the verge of extinction, from which it has never fully recovered. Today only a few thousand survive in scattered colonies;

And more recently, the Norwegian ice-breaker *Polarhav* made an exploratory expedition to the Antarctic in 1964 and took 1,100 crabeater and leopard seals.

Norway has the largest sealing industry in the world, and is naturally concerned about the possible cessation of north-west Atlantic sealing by 1975, and by the catch limits already imposed on the Western Ice (Jan Mayen), 87

Population of the Harp Seal

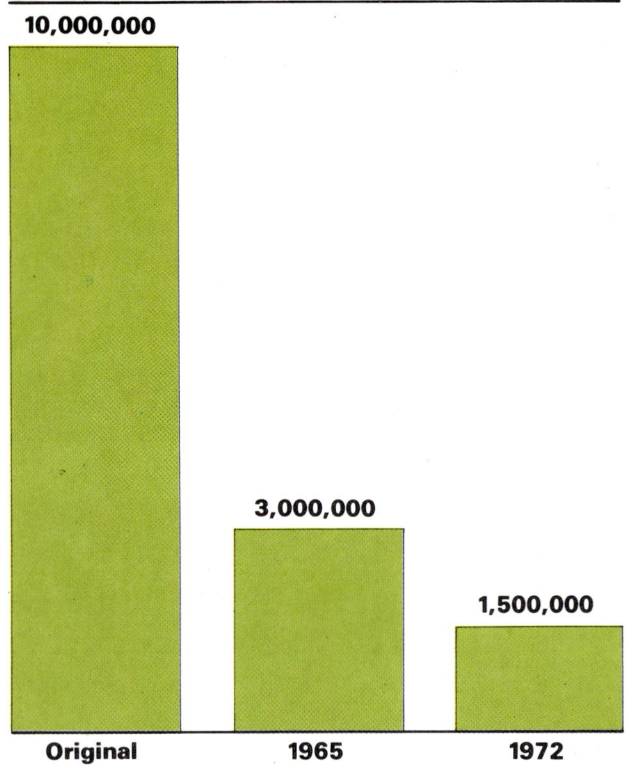

GROWTH CYCLE OF THE HARP SEAL

Age	Stage	Appearance	Behaviour
Birth –10 days	'Whitecoat'	Whitish-yellow	Period of lactation
10–21 days	'Ragged-jacket'	As above, but mottled gray	Fully weaned and abandoned by mother
21–28 days	'Beater'	Mottled dark gray top, white underside	Molt complete and swimming
1–4 years	'Bedlammer', or 'Immature'	Dark gray with broken brown markings	Accompanies mature seals on migrations
4–6 years	'Harp seal', or 'Adult'	Light gray, with dark brown 'harp' design on back'	Age of puberty occurs in this period

and on the Eastern Ice (Novaya Zemla and White Sea). Norwegian commercial interests do hope to have a sealing operation established in the Antarctic by 1975, and therefore I believe it would be extremely irresponsible to allow the Antarctic to be opened up like this without agreeing effective safeguards for the seals' welfare and conservation. The convention agreed by the Antarctic Treaty nations was an attempt to do just this—but many conservationists are doubtful whether the safeguards are adequate. The more important provisions are as follows:

1. Three areas, which are either seal breeding grounds or are subject to long-term scientific research programs, have been declared reserves. It is therefore forbidden to capture or kill seals in the South Orkney Islands, the south-western Ross Sea, and Edisto Inlet and an area west of a line from Cape Hallet to Helm Point.
2. Seals may not be captured or killed during the closed season from 1 March to 31 August inclusive.
3. The whole area has been divided into six numbered zones which will be closed in numerical order between 1 September and the last day of February.
4. The maximum permissible annual catch is: crabeater seal (*Lobodon carcinophagus*)—175,000; leopard seal (*Hydrurga leptonyx*)—12,000; and Weddell seal (*Leptonychotes weddelli*)—5,000.
5. Weddell seals of one year and older must not be taken between 1 September and 31 January (the breeding period).
6. Catch quotas will be reviewed in the light of scientific assessments.
7. The following species have been declared fully protected: Ross seal (*Ommatophoca rossi*), southern elephant seal (*Mirounga leonina*), and fur seals of the genus *Arctocephalus*.
8. Other provisions of the convention call for an exchange of scientific data; declarations of numbers, sex, and age group taken; and details of vessels involved.

These are the main conservation safeguards of the new convention, and only time and experience will show how effective they are. In my opinion there are many omissions, and too much is left to chance. One might justifiably ask whose statistics were used to determine the sustainable yields of crabeater, Weddell, and leopard seals. How accurate and recent is this information? Who will enforce the provisions? Why did the participating nations fail to agree on an effective observer scheme?

Japan is a prominent member of the International Whaling Commission, and is known to operate whale catchers under a flag of convenience; she is also an Antarctic Treaty nation, and has an active sealing industry. With three of the six species of Antarctic seals protected, and two others with low sustainable yields, the margin for error is slight. Illicit sealing operations could have disastrous results.

The Antarctic seal convention is not without its critics, and the American delegation had strong reservations about signing it. But although it is admittedly far from perfect, I don't think it should be condemned outright. The aim was to lay down a foundation on which sound conservation policy can be built. With reasonable goodwill by the sealing nations, and a determination not to repeat the mistakes of the past, the survival of the Antarctic seals could be assured.

Mother harp seal with her young *(above)*, known as a 'whitecoat'. The young seals are born on sea ice during the first week of March, but grow quickly and are fully weaned after about 10 days. It is these whitecoats that the sealers hunt *(right)*. Cruel though it looks, this method of killing the young seals is generally considered humane—providing the club is the correct size and weight, and is used properly.

Nicole Duplaix-Hall

The Sea Otter Success Story

Demand for sea otter fur—once considered the most valuable fur in the world—has declined to such an extent that it is no longer worth selling it. What was probably the last public sale of sea otter pelts took place in Seattle in February 1972. This erosion in demand, coupled with the remarkable recovery in numbers of the sea otter from near extinction in 1910 to its present total of some 50,000, adds up to perhaps the most dramatic conservation success story this century.

Before examining its over-exploitation and subsequent recovery, let us take a look at the way of life of this charming marine mammal. The most un-otter-like of the otters, the sea otter (*Enhydra lutris*) is almost exclusively marine, venturing ashore only to give birth and, in undisturbed areas, to sleep. The massive head and short blunt face, with its large nose pad, is much paler than the body. Coloration varies from brown to almost black, and the soft underfur is sparsely covered with long guard hairs. Unlike other members of the mustelid family, it has no scent glands, and, unlike other otters, it has a short tail and small compact forepaws with partially retractile claws. The sea otter's thickly webbed, flattened hind paws have an elongated fifth digit, a feature unique among mammals, which helps in paddling while on its back (on the surface) or on its front (underwater). Adults may reach a little over five feet in length, including the twelve-inch tail and weigh anywhere between sixty-five and a hundred pounds depending on the season and the availability of food. Its molars are broad and rounded, lacking the sharp cusps found in other carnivores but perfectly adapted to crushing abrasive mussels, sea urchins, and tough squids.

Sea otters are social animals and live in closely knit groups. No strict hierarchy prevails as in primate troops and very little aggressive behavior is observed. Often separate male and female groups exist. Periodically a male will leave his group in search of a female, or a female may leave hers in search of a mate. Copulation takes place in the water or, less commonly, on land. The couple remain together a few days, then go their different ways.

Cubs are born throughout the year with a peak season during the more clement summer months. The cub (rarely twins) is born in a more advanced state of development than any other mustelid, eyes open, well furred, with a complete set of milk teeth. While floating on her back, the mother holds the cub clasped to her chest with her forepaws. When she dives for food, the cub will remain helpless, bobbing like a cork on the surface or attempting a few unco-ordinated paddling strokes until she returns to retrieve it. When suddenly alarmed by a boat or a predator, the mother grips the cub's neck in her teeth and dives with it. Such a desperate move may prove fatal to the young cub if she cannot surface within half a minute. After two or three months, the cub has learned to swim and dive but will remain by its mother's side for over a year, often two. She watches over it constantly,

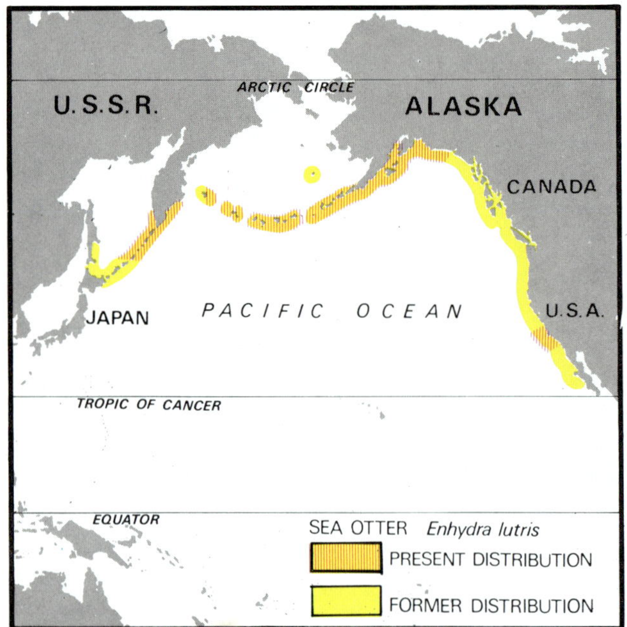

rarely allowing it to stray and indeed hunters used to report mothers following them fearlessly when they kidnapped the young ones. Like monkeys, sea otters may clasp and groom their dead infants for days before abandoning them. Such single-minded solicitude is rare among marine mammals. A close mother-young relationship is vital in sea otters because a juvenile cannot remain underwater long enough to gather sufficient food on its own until the end of its first year. If it became permanently separated from its only reliable food source, its mother, it would surely not survive.

In the wild sea otters spend most of their waking hours feeding and grooming in peaceful groups. They begin shortly after dawn, diving 30 to 120 feet in calm waters, half a mile offshore, returning to the surface after a few minutes. Surprisingly enough they do not pry mussels from the rocks with their teeth but with their forepaws. Probably the most remarkable feature of the sea otter's behavioral repertoire, however, is its tool-using behavior. While floating on its back it will rapidly pound a clam on its chest until the shell is broken. Then tucking its anvil in a loose fold of skin under its forearm, it will dive again. Favorite anvils or bits of food can be held under the armpits quite securely when swimming or grooming. Even in captivity, when given soft food, the sea otter will continue this activity, sometimes uselessly pounding a stone against the edge of the pool. How did this habit among sea otters originate? Was it a consequence of frustration when even the strongest teeth could not crush hard clams, nor dexterous paws prize the edges open? Freshwater otters, particularly the Asiatic small-clawed otter (*Amblonyx cinerea*) and the African clawless otter (*Aonyx capensis*), will use tools in captivity to lever open doors or shift heavy drain covers. So tool-using may be more widespread in otters than has been previously

Scientific researcher with sea otter at Amchitka Island, Alaska, one of the animal's present strongholds.

thought. Perhaps tool-using in sea otters is yet another adaptation which an animal, originally terrestrial, had to make to meet the requirements of a new and alien environment.

Sea otters, unlike seals or whales, do not possess a thick layer of insulating blubber. Instead they rely for warmth on a layer of air trapped in the underfur which stops the water from reaching the skin. Once the under-fur is soiled by food particles, or an oil slick, or is tousled by rough waters, the air shield is broken and the fur loses its waterproofing qualities. A waterlogged sea otter lacks buoyancy and finds it difficult to keep afloat—and will quickly succumb to the numbing cold of the Pacific waters. To avoid this danger, the otter must spend long hours every day grooming its fur energetically while floating near its companions or resting on the beach. The fur is washed, rubbed, and kneaded together between the forepaws; nibbled with the incisors; or rubbed against rocks or another otter. Grooming is one of the first things the sea otter does upon waking and the last before going to sleep.

When a sea otter is unable to feed and groom because

Population of the Sea Otter

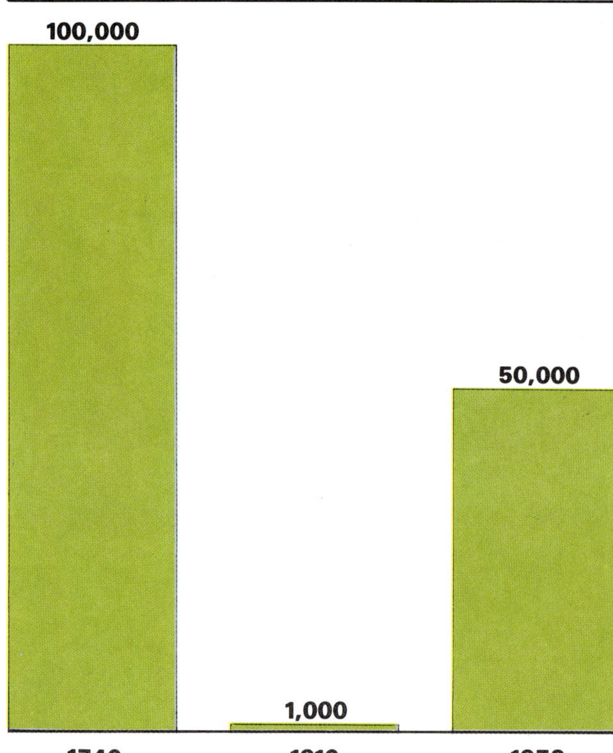

of human disturbance, a severe storm, or in overpopulated areas where the food sources are depleted, it is virtually doomed unless it can resume these activities within twenty-four hours. The sea otter needs to eat about 20 per cent of its own weight every day to provide the energy necessary to maintain a steady body temperature in a cold marine habitat.

The truth of the matter is that the sea otter is probably too specialized for its own good. It can only exploit a narrow littoral zone because it needs the protection of sheltered bays, and because it can dive only so deep for its food. Its only natural enemies are sharks, killer whales, and, in Alaska, the bald eagle. But these take an insignificant toll. In fact it is only its habitat, the sea, which regulates sea otter numbers now that man appears to have put away his club. Winter and spring storms kill many juvenile and elderly sea otters, particularly in areas where the animals are too numerous for the food available. These two age groups are not resilient enough to face the rigors of storms at sea and die of stress and starvation within a few days.

When Steller discovered the sea otter in 1741, the world population was probably around 100,000 individuals. They ranged along the Pacific Coast from the Kurile Islands north of Japan, past the Kamchatka Peninsula, along the Aleutian Islands chain under the Bering Straits, and down the Alaskan and Canadian coast to northern Mexico. Unfortunately, man's greed was to change this state of affairs dramatically. Russian,

Japanese, Chinese, British and American fur hunters ruthlessly clubbed hundreds of thousands of sea otters to death for their exquisite fur. Soon the smallest marine mammal was headed for extinction—a route that the largest, the blue whale, was later to follow.

By 1840, sea otters had become so rare that hunting was no longer a commercial proposition. In 1910, when only 1,000 or 2,000 were left, an international treaty banned all hunting. But by then, most scientists agreed that the species would probably soon be extinct. However, small groups of sea otters remained in the Kurile islands, the Aleutians, and off California. Fourteen were seen off Monterey, California in 1914, but this information was kept secret until 1938 when they were officially 're-discovered' north of Point Sur, between San Francisco and Los Angeles, by a zoologist who estimated their number at around 100. The population grew at 5 per cent a year, and they began to spread up and down the California coast. Now they are believed to number at least 1,000. Poaching by the abalone fishermen, who accuse the sea otter of depleting their catches, and pollution, will probably maintain the number at about this level.

Meanwhile the sea otters were also making a comeback on Amchitka Island in the Aleutians near Alaska. Because theirs was a particularly favorable habitat, the population growth was more rapid—about 10 to 20 per cent a year. When the density reached forty sea otters per square mile, there was a sudden crash in numbers due to depleted food supplied. Why didn't this population split up and move to other available habitats and food resources? Probably for several ecological and behavioral reasons: because of the wide stretches of open sea between hospitable islands where the otters did not venture; because there was no seasonal migration during the lean winter months; because the animal's sedentary tendencies caused it to remain in a limited home range until extreme overcrowding forced segments of the population to emigrate, often too late. Pollution in coastal industrial areas may also provide yet another effective ecological barrier in Canada and California—no such animal can live in a sewer.

Slowly the depleted numbers of these northern sea otters rose from ten to fifteen per square mile, where they stand today. Total numbers are now estimated to be nearly 45,000—and could increase to 70,000 if the otters repopulate unused habitats. The late-1971 underground explosion of a nuclear device on Amchitka Island probably killed 1,000 to 1,350 animals in subsequent landslides, tidal waves and storms. Although an extremely unfortunate occurrence, this man-made cataclysm will not permanently affect sea otter numbers in that area. The rate of population increase varies according to the density of animals, which in turn is regulated by the availability of food. And in the rich Alaskan waters one can estimate sixteen cubs per hundred adult sea otters per year—which is very promising.

*Northern sea otters on land in Alaska **(left)**—a rare sight, as this marine mammal spends most of its time at sea. The sea otters **(below)** resting amongst the kelp are two out of about 1,000 of the southern group, found along the coast of California. Regular grooming is a vital aspect of the sea otter's daily routine **(above)**. Unlike seals and whales, the sea otter does not have a layer of insulating blubber, relying instead on air trapped in its underfur to keep it afloat and warm. The animals spend hours every day energetically grooming their fur so that it maintains its waterproofing qualities.*

Finally, the skin harvest. Small numbers of Alaskan sea otters have been taken by Government biologists between 1962 and 1970, and their skins sold in Seattle between 1968 and 1972. The total sold was 2,725, at an average price of $134.96 (£54). But the last sale took place on 9 February 1972 on the Seattle Fur Exchange, and Alaskan State officials now consider that the profit margin is too small to be worthwhile. It has been suggested that private individuals be licensed to take sea otters for sale, but so far no such authorization has been given.

Why has the sea otter—frequently described as the most valuable fur in the world—gone out of fashion? Among the reasons cited is the fact that the fur has been taken off the market for so long that potential buyers don't know what it is; that the fur is too heavy for today's purposes; that conservationists have encouraged the belief that the sea otter is an endangered species; and that there is a growing feeling among an increasingly urban population that it is wrong to take wild animals for their skins. Whatever the reason it is clear that the sea otter benefits.

The best current estimate of the world population of sea otter, taking into account the 5,300 Russian animals, is about 50,000. Still only half what it was in 1741. But we can hope that, given time, the sea otter will return to even more of its old haunts and remain, unmolested, as an important and attractive member of the marine fauna of the North Pacific. There is no reason why this conservation success should not be permanent.

REPTILES AND AMPHIBIANS

Despite Federal protection, the Mississippi alligator is still widely poached; these are at a pool in Florida.

Poachers Still Hunt the Alligator

Giant Tortoises

George Laycock

Poachers Still Hunt the Alligator

When the Endangered Species Conservation Act became fully effective in June 1970, conservationists everywhere hoped that the beleaguered American alligator was at last getting a reprieve. With the ancient reptilian given this added measure of federal protection, perhaps the illegal hide market would dry up and the incessant alligator poaching come to a halt.

Soon state wildlife officials across the South-east were announcing that the alligator had indeed been saved. News releases came from state game and fish departments telling of the remarkable comeback of the alligator. The stories went like this: Faced with the threat of federal prosecution, plus constant pursuit by state wildlife officers, sad and disillusioned poachers, young and old, were sloshing out of the swamps to hang up their alligator-killing tools—their hatchets, hooks, and guns—and saying farewell to a lucrative way of life.

Then came talk of removing the alligator from the endangered species list soon so the surplus animals could be cropped in an annual harvest. Both Louisiana and Florida officials hoped this would lead to a thriving hide industry with skins sent to market through legal channels.

Meanwhile, out in the swamps, the alligators noticed very little change in the tempo of man's attack on their numbers. The reason is that the poaching went right on despite the new federal legislation.

This was clearly borne out on 3 April 1972, in a federal courtroom in Atlanta, Georgia. On that date a grand jury indicted 47-year-old Quince Clayton Plott and his son, Christopher Joel Plott, on forty counts of illegal buying, selling, and transporting of 6,294 alligator skins. The penalties for each, if they were convicted, could have totalled forty years in prison and $400,000 (£160,000) in fines.

The Georgia indictment was not the first case against the senior Plott. A New York City grand jury had also charged him with illegally shipping more than 4,788 alligator hides valued at some $92,000 (£37,000) into New York. He also faced similar charges in another Georgia federal court. Eventually, both father and son were tried in New York in the summer of 1972. Some seventy counts in several states were lumped together—and both Plotts pleaded guilty. The sentences handed out were strangely lenient: six months in prison for the father and two months for the son. In addition, both were put on probation for five years. But the judge ordered that the sentences were not to be concurrent—so that the family business would not suffer unduly. Despite the light sentences, the trial has probably dampened other poachers' ardor, even if only temporarily, and the details of the case make fascinating reading.

The charges were the result of a persistent two-year investigation by federal game management agents, who identified Plott as a prime figure in a network of 460 poachers, transporters, and dealers illegally engaged in the alligator hide business in seven south-eastern states. Between 1968 and 1971 this ring, according to federal

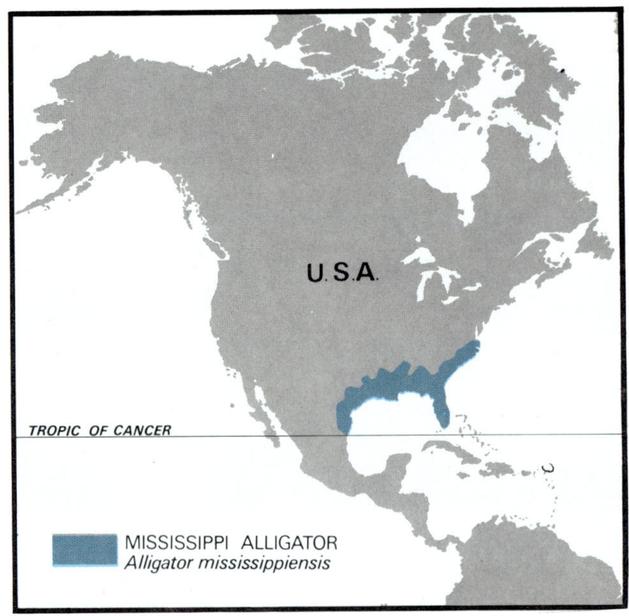

agents, killed and brought to market at least 127,000 alligators valued at more than $4,140,000 (£1,656,000). Tentacles of this criminal network reached around the world into several countries where there is a demand for American alligator hides. This promised to become the biggest wildlife law enforcement case in history.

Trouble started for Q. C. Plott in December 1969 when federal game management agent William R. Kensinger transferred from his Chesapeake Bay post to become the Bureau of Sport Fisheries and Wildlife's agent in charge for the state of Georgia. Within a month Kensinger began hearing rumors that Plott was trafficking in alligator skins. Some informants believed Plott had as many as $50,000 (£20,000) worth of hides on hand at a time. Kensinger also learned that in October 1969, some months after Georgia had halted all legal killing of alligators, Plott had made an unsuccessful attempt in court to block enforcement of the new law.

Kensinger and his supervisor, Frederick A. Williams, working with other federal and state game agents in Florida, Georgia, and south-east Texas, furnished descriptions of Plott's vehicles on the theory that they might be used in the illegal transport of hides across state borders. But neither Plott's two vans nor his pickup camper nor the personal cars driven by the father and son were spotted outside Georgia.

Next, Kensinger decided to check the ports where hides might be shipped by boat to foreign destinations. He asked federal game management agent Willard J. Frazier to investigate the port of Savannah, closest to Atlanta and most convenient for Plott. Frazier went first to the US Customs officer. The Customs records showed that Plott had openly exported alligator skins—clearly labeled as such—after it became illegal in Georgia, and continued to do so even after enactment of the federal law.

This series of photographs shows how alligator poachers operate. Sometimes the poachers cruise slowly through the swamps under cover of night, picking out the gleaming eyes of their prey with a flashlight. Then, moving closer, they kill it with rifle, shotgun, or hatchet. Other times, alligators are caught on turtle hooks baited with rotting meat. Young animals are preferred. Sometimes the poachers are caught by law enforcement officers, but unfortunately not often enough.

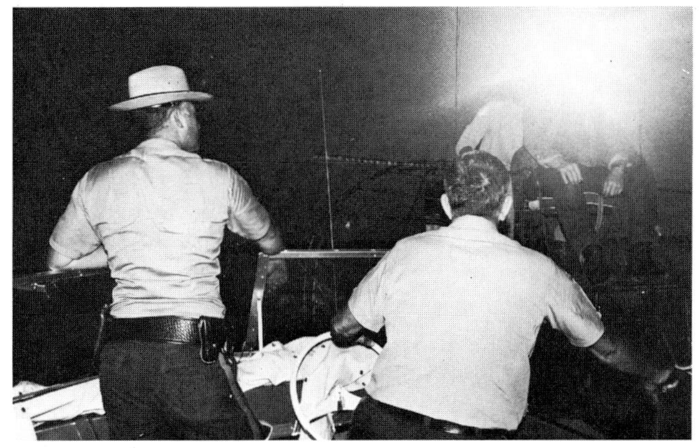

Frazier acquired nineteen documents detailing recent shipments by Plott of containers still clearly labeled as alligator hides. Within the containers, according to the documents, were 6,545 skins valued at $152,784.55 (£61,100). Although Plott still did not know it, the net was beginning to tighten.

On 1 April 1971, the Customs officer at Savannah contacted Frazier and told him that a shipment labeled 'small scale crocodiles' was aboard a Japanese freighter scheduled to depart for Tokyo within two hours. Kensinger cabled the American embassy in Tokyo and had the shipment seized at Yokohama and returned.

On the next shipment, Kensinger's tip came somewhat earlier and there was time to move. Customs notified him that a shipment of skins from Plott was on the dock headed for Tokyo. That night he called Dr F. Wayne King, curator of herpetology for the New York Zoological Society. The following morning Dr King, a federal game agent, and the senior resident agent for US Customs opened the three barrels in Plott's shipment and examined the contents piece by piece. In the barrels were 345 skins. Said Dr King's affidavit: 'The barrels contained the raw salted hides of American alligators (*Alligator mississippiensis*).'

Now the federal agents could act. Killing and shipping the alligators had broken both state and federal laws. The Endangered Species Conservation Act had been in force for nearly a year, and even old hides taken prior to its passage could not have been legally shipped. But the skins seized, as Dr King pointed out, had been taken in recent months: 'The bits of fat and flesh adhering to the inside of the hides were still fresh, and neither dehydrated from salt, nor discolored from drying.'

Four days later, armed with federal search warrants, teams of game agents simultaneously descended on the Q. C. Plott Raw Fur and Ginseng Company as well as a customs broker, George W. Wise Jr., and the Brown Transport Corporation, both in Savannah, Georgia. They seized cartons of records from all three firms and hauled them back to their office on Peachtree Street. That night Kensinger and another agent, Harold Steele, began making a microfilm record of every document. At the end of thirty-six hours they had photographed more than 5,700 papers, including accounting records, correspondence, and canceled checks.

These records were remarkably detailed. Whenever Plott bought hides he logged the names, addresses, numbers, and sizes of the hides, and amounts paid for them. As Kensinger and Steele filmed the documents, they also began extracting a list of suspects, which was turned over to a bureau undercover agent. In the following weeks the undercover agent visited dozens of these illicit operators, most of them alligator poachers, confirming evidence and adding new names to the list of people involved.

Kensinger also acquired a grand jury subpoena, enabling him to obtain the telephone toll receipts of the Plott company. This added corroborative evidence plus new names for the growing list. Very carefully, the federal agents were constructing a solid case. And in the course of unraveling this sordid operation, they identified thirteen companies plus four brokers dealing in alligator hides in New York, prepared affidavits for search warrants, and relayed these to game agents in that city. Other search warrants were served on leading dealers in Florida and Louisiana, plus a major exporter of alligator skins in New Jersey.

Q. C. Plott was not taking all this quietly. The seizure of his records had slowed his business considerably. In a letter to President Nixon he protested that the federal agents were attempting to put a 23-year-old family enterprise out of business. 'As you know,' he wrote, 'the fur and skin trade is the oldest trade in this nation. It began years ago with the first white men exchanging novelties for skins with the Indians. Now the great "ecology craze" groups are attempting to change a trade which has existed for many, many years.' In one telephone conversation, he is quoted as telling a federal game agent that the country is in trouble because a bunch of 'Commie conservationists' pushed the Endangered Species Conservation Act through Congress, and that he intended to stay in the hide business—legally or illegally.

Most of Plott's shipments had gone to one Japanese firm, Inoue and Company, Ltd, of Tokyo. Other shippers are known to have supplied large numbers of alligator hides to buyers in Italy, Spain, France, and England. For the past several years the price of raw alligator hides has been five dollars or more per foot. The prime hides for use in the making of such products as alligator bags, shoes, belts, and wallets come from animals three to five feet in length, with the finest hides of all said to come from Louisiana.

The alligators are slaughtered under cover of night. Historically, the favored method of the 'gator killers has been to cruise slowly in a boat, shining a light over the water until it picks up the ruby gleam reflected by an alligator's eyes. Then, while the creature stares back into the light, the boat moves closer. Finally the alligator is killed with a .22 caliber rifle, a shotgun, or a hatchet. Others are caught on turtle hooks baited with rotting meat and suspended a few inches above the water, where the turtles can't reach but the alligators can.

Before the skin is removed, an incision is hacked in the base of the tail and a long stiff wire run the length of the spinal column. This stops the dying animal from thrashing around in the boat. The stripped skins are then salted and rolled to preserve them.

Hide transactions take place in secrecy. Shipments of skins are delivered to pickup agents who, in turn, haul them—usually in the trunks of their automobiles—to dealers who have contacts with tanneries both in the United States and abroad.

Nobody knows how many alligators are killed every year to supply the leather trade in various parts of the

Despite its rather awesome appearance the alligator seldom poses any danger to man. In fact, its presence is generally beneficial. For instance, alligators love to wallow in swamps, and as they dig into the damp soil with their feet and tail they form shallow pools where freshwater fishes can spawn and develop. Many of these fishes feed voraciously on mosquito larvae—and so the alligator indirectly keeps down the mosquito population.

world. One federal agent estimates that the 127,000 hides tabulated in the Plott case make up perhaps one-fourth of the kill. If so, half a million alligators have gone illegally to the hide business since 1968. Although today's biggest populations of alligators are found in Florida and Louisiana, the federal agents have traced alligator poaching to Georgia, South Carolina, North Carolina, Texas, Alabama, and Mississippi.

Presumably it is in Florida and Louisiana that the often heralded alligator 'farming' scheme would flourish if the reptile were ever removed from the endangered species list and permits were granted to raise alligators in captivity and legally market their hides. But disclosure of such continued large-scale poaching, despite recently strengthened laws, weakens at least two arguments advanced by the advocates of alligator farming. First is the basic question of whether the species, as claimed by some, is out of danger. Evidence indicates it is not, except perhaps locally. Second, arguments that poaching has been stopped, or even substantially slowed, are no longer meaningful. There seems little justification, indeed, for removing the alligator from the endangered species list.

Likewise, the arrogance of the hide buyers and the persistence of the poachers contradict the reasoning behind one proposal for a system of tagging or belly-marking that presumably would assure that only legal skins from 'farmed' alligators would enter the channels of commerce. The idea is to identify domestically produced alligators by recording their 'belly-prints'—prints said to be as individual as human fingerprints. Every skin sent to market would thus be identifiable. Supposedly, this technique would stop all poaching because dealing in undocumented hides would be illegal.

Alligator poachers, however, have always dealt in unmarked hides. Nor have they hesitated to break the law, and one wonders how a belly-printing system would alter their ethical standards.

Federal agents know that bringing the Plott case to trial will not end the alligator poaching problem. 'Slow it down for a while, maybe,' was the way one of them stated it. 'But there is simply too much money involved, and when you shut it off in one place, sooner or later it is going to crop up somewhere else.'

What fascinates the agents is the boldness and arrogance of those who deal illegally in the hides of these endangered creatures. Kensinger, Fred Williams, and their fellow officers are still amazed at their fortune in uncovering the cache of documents giving detailed information on the Plott enterprise. They also are convinced that as pressure increases the hide buyers will find new and more secretive ways of handling their product. 'We think there is an increasing trend,' one agent said, 'to deal only in cash. Such dealings can't be traced easily by us or the Internal Revenue Service.' Neither can dealers be expected to attempt any longer to ship clearly labeled alligator skins through commercial channels. Probably hides are already being smuggled out of the country to other places in this hemisphere for trans-shipping overseas.

Where does all this leave the American alligator? The chances seem excellent that this latest legal action has slowed down the poaching. But the federal agents harbor no illusions. They fully expect the outlaws to stay in business because of the big money involved.

Catching an alligator poacher at work is one of the most difficult of all law enforcement jobs. The big cases such as the Plott affair can be more effective. But even more important is the elimination of the markets and putting the buyers out of business. Then, the poaching will stop.

Giant Tortoises

Tony Beamish

Giant Tortoises on Aldabra

A few years ago practically no-one had heard of Aldabra, a large coral atoll in the western Indian Ocean, but not much more than a speck on most people's atlases. However, it hit the headlines in Britain and America when plans were announced to turn it into a military staging post for the RAF. British and American conservationists, and bird-lovers in particular, waged a relentless campaign to save this island—a scientific treasure house, and one of the very few unspoiled islands in the tropics. Fortunately Aldabra was spared, not because of the scientific arguments (of which there were many) but because the British economy at the time could not stand the expense of constructing the airfield.

Aldabra is a haven for birds of many kinds, but it is also the home of many unique animals and plants of other kinds. Above all, it is the last home—indeed stronghold —of the Indian Ocean giant tortoise. Once found in various Indian Ocean islands, it is now confined to this one large atoll.

Parts of Aldabra present an astonishing sight around midday. Under the scattered trees and larger bushes that offer shade from the scorching equatorial sun the giant reptiles can be seen stacked sometimes three deep. I have counted as many as fifty sheltering under a single tree. There is no sound at all except for the occasional scraping of shells as a tortoise slides into a better position. Here and there a green gecko darts over the recumbent bodies. In the presence of these multitudes it amazed me to think that not long ago several reputable scientists reported that the giant tortoise was near extinction on Aldabra.

In fact, the latest information of the population of this species makes some of the best conservation news for a long time. In 1968 an expedition that surveyed all four islands of the atoll rim—over seventy miles in circumference—as well as the larger islands in the lagoon itself, reported that the tortoise population of Aldabra might be as high as 80,000, many times that of its hard-pressed cousin far away in the Galapagos Islands of the Pacific.

One possible explanation of this startling discrepancy in the reports is that most of the tortoises live at the east end of South Island, a long way from the settlement and the only safe landing place. Here there are only a few tortoises to be seen, mostly youngsters of thirty years or less. The larger animals who may once have lived in this area are probably now to be seen in zoos. In recent years, lessees of Aldabra have been allowed by the Seychelles Government to export to zoos a certain number of tor-

toises every year . . . and the larger the animal the higher the price. It is no easy task to hump a 250-pound animal across razor-sharp and honeycombed coral rock, so they obviously took those nearest to hand.

But this cropping is now a thing of the past, for Aldabra, well described as a living natural history museum almost undisturbed by man, is now firmly in the hands of Britain's Royal Society and probably safe for all time. A fine new research station with living accommodation for visiting scientists and research workers shines whitely at the mouth of West Channel, cheering evidence of a great conservation victory. The threat, once so close, that an airfield might be built has now receded almost to nothing. Though it should not be forgotten that as long as the relevant Anglo-American treaty remains in force there is still a danger.

A long-term conservation program is now under way for the tortoises, and the few tourists who occasionally visit the atoll can see a number of the animals marked with a titanium disc inset into the back of the carapace or shell. Jack Frazier, a herpetologist who studied Aldabra's wildlife in 1970 and 1971, told me about some of his

Giant tortoises on Aldabra of three different sizes (and thus of three different ages). They were positioned like this by the photographer, who returned them to the ground later; they would never normally travel in this way.

observations, such as the extraordinary slowness of their digestive process (it takes about thirty days for food to pass through the body). A visitor to Aldabra several years earlier once saw a tortoise devouring a can of green paint. I have myself often remarked what undiscriminating eaters these reptiles are, consuming with apparent relish such diverse fodder as paper and vitamin pills.

Everything about the adult giants is slow and deliberate, but contrary to popular belief they do sometimes fight, usually two males over a female. Their attitude to human intruders is one of caution; as you approach they withdraw into their huge shells and swivel, hissing softly. If, however, you are sitting quietly in camp they will come close with no sign of fear to investigate and forage. Very few baby tortoises are to be seen; this is probably because the main breeding area is away from the feeding grounds on the flat rockland, called *platin* in Creole, and partly because the young tortoises are surprisingly swift on their feet and adept at hiding in the low scrub. After the rains when the rock pools are full of fresh water, tortoises can be seen every evening swimming easily in search of water weed. Clearly the animal must be a good swimmer, despite his great weight and density, to have reached the atoll in the first place, but you do not normally see this land animal in the sea. I was surprised, therefore, one day in March 1971 to see a tortoise deliberately enter the sea at the southern mouth of West Channel and swim confidently across 300 yards of water to one of the small islands. The imperative would most likely have been food.

In the dry season it seems that food is scarce; favored trees have tortoise crop-lines and you can observe animals climbing on each others' backs to reach the green leaves at the full extent of their long necks. The only competition for food supply comes from several herds of feral goats, bred from animals released by the first lessee, but this is not believed to be serious. The giant tortoise has no enemy on Aldabra, except for man in the old days. Unfortunately, tortoise meat is good to eat and the creature was an ideal package of fresh meat for sailors before the days of refrigeration—which is one reason why Aldabra is today their only remaining wild home. But at least it is a safe one for an endangered species—and there are precious few places you can say that about.

Roger Perry

Giant Tortoises on the Galápagos

The famous tortoises of the Galápagos have excited man's imagination ever since the islands were discovered in 1535. Their extraordinary abundance on these dry volcanic islands seemed somehow to defy the very laws of nature. So numerous were they, claimed an early writer, that in places it would have been possible to travel simply by stepping from one giant shell to another.

But even more extraordinary than their sheer numbers and size was the fact that there were different kinds of tortoises on different islands. Fifteen races were identified, and ten of these were living on separate islands. The other five kinds were found (and are still found) on Albemarle (Isabela), the largest of the Galápagos islands—each of them having evolved in the seclusion of one of the five principal volcanoes which have united to form the island. The majority of these tortoises can be told apart by their size, shape, and in some cases, the color of their shells: small deviations perhaps, or at any rate superficial, but of immense evolutionary significance. Differences between the tortoises of various islands greatly impressed the young Charles Darwin during his visit to the Galápagos in 1835, and his observations there were to lead him on to his long searching enquiry into the origin of species. 'I never dreamed,' he wrote, 'that islands about fifty or sixty miles apart . . . would have been differently tenanted.'

To those interested in wildlife and wild places the encouraging news today is that the great majority of these races—at least eleven of the original fifteen—still survive. A few years ago this would have been rated impossible.

Since the beginning of the nineteenth century, when the British and North American whaling fleets moved into the Pacific, the giant tortoises had been systematically exterminated—a massacre that hardly abated until the scarcity of the animals themselves made exploitation uneconomic. It was no secret that these huge reptiles could survive long periods without food or water—an ability that has been decisive in their long association with these arid islands. Now, ironically, it was to spell their doom; for in those days of voyaging under sail there was no way of preserving fresh food and meat on board. So the giant tortoises, which were tasty and had the great virtue of remaining alive for as long as a year in

Tortoise on typical Aldabran lava rock. The conditions are harsh on Aldabra, and it is probably true that if the tortoises had been able to choose, they would not have chosen this as their last refuge.

103

the holds of ships, became a valuable commodity. Even when uncontrolled slaughter had driven the whalers out of business, other dangers arose, particularly from settlers and introduced animals. By the middle of the present century it was feared that half a dozen races had disappeared, and all the others were far along the road to extinction.

Fortunately, the inhospitable terrain had prevented easy access to all but a few of the islands. Many parts remained virtually unknown until recent years and the establishment of a permanent biological station in the islands under an international organization called the Charles Darwin Foundation for the Galápagos Isles. Then, with surveys initiated by personnel of the station, a rather more hopeful picture began to emerge. Viable populations of first one and then another race were found to be surviving.

The existence of the Chatham Island (San Cristóbal) tortoise (which by the turn of the century was assumed to be near extinction) was confirmed in 1965 by an Ecuadorian conservation official Miguel Castro. By the latest count 153 individuals have been found and marked (by a numerical system of notching the marginal plates of the shell, or carapace).

Tortoise nesting-areas have been located on Duncan (Pinzón), James (Santiago) and on the rugged volcanoes of Albemarle. Apart from Duncan Island, where 103 animals have been marked, the population of all these races are in the hundreds. That of Volcán Alcedo, the most central of Albemarle's volcanoes, has been estimated as high as 3,000.

For many years it was thought unlikely that any tortoises remained on Hood (Española), the dry low-lying island in the south-east of the archipelago and best known as the only nesting-site of the waved albatross.

Then, in 1963, a single tortoise was discovered disconsolately munching cactus pads in the company of fifteen goats. Over the next eight years, ten further tortoises were found on this island, probably representing the grand total of adults remaining of this quite distinctive race.

More recently, in March 1972, the tortoise-researchers learned of perhaps the most surprising find of all: the re-discovery of the Abingdon (Pinta) race. It had been thought that this small goat-infested island had been thoroughly searched; yet, apparently, not one but several survivors had escaped the notice of National Park officials. Tracks of several have been found; so one may hope that both sexes are still represented on the island, and the search continues.

This last discovery also means that, despite gloomy predictions since the beginning of the century, no Galápagos tortoises seem to have become extinct during the past hundred years. The Charles Island (Floreana) race disappeared not many years after Darwin's visit, and the Barrington (Santa Fe) tortoise probably went before the 1860s; insufficient material has been found to substantiate the validity of the race described from Jervis (Rábida).

But encouraging as all this is, it does not detract from the fact that all the tortoise races are still threatened in one way or another. Hunting for meat and oil, although banned by the Ecuadorian Government, continues sporadically, and there seems no end to the problems caused by man and especially his companions—dogs, cats, rats, pigs, and goats, all tragically brought at one time or another and turned loose on the islands. Programs were started during the 1960s to control the worst of these feral animals. The Ecuadorian Government, UNESCO, the International Union for Conservation of Nature, the World Wildlife Fund, and many national

*Miguel Castro measures eggs of giant tortoises on Duncan Island in the Galápagos **(far left)**. He will then collect them and take them to the hatchery at the Charles Darwin Research Station on Indefatigable Island (the incubator **(left)** is seen at Darwin Station.) The experiment was successful in the case of the Duncan tortoises, and the first batch of young animals was returned in December 1970.*

*The Galápagos problem. Giant tortoise with wild donkeys (**above**) at the pool by the geyser on the slope of Volcan Alcedo, Albemarle Island. Though this particular population of tortoises is quite numerous, the donkeys represent a threat—though not such a great threat as other introduced animals, like cats, rats, pigs, and goats.*

organizations and individuals have given support to this work, which continues under competent officials of the Galápagos National Park Service. Already, goats have been successfully eradicated from the badly over-run island of Barrington—too late to do much for the tortoise, but this will allow the vegetation to recover and benefit other endemic wildlife.

Even with these measures in hand, additional steps are still required to help the more seriously threatened races of tortoises. One way, perhaps the best, lies in establishing breeding stocks at the Darwin Station on Indefatigable Island (Santa Cruz), with a view to re-introducing populations of young animals when these are of an age better able to withstand the hazards of their natural environment. This project began modestly in 1965.

On the island of Duncan there is the problem of black rats (introduced from sailing ships many years ago), which dig into the nests and kill the tiny, defenseless hatchlings. An attempt was therefore made to incubate eggs brought from this island and to rear the young in converted bird cages at the station. The experiment

*Unusual view **(left)** of mating pair of Galápagos giant tortoises; these are on Albemarle Island, at the rim of the largest crater. Of the ten races of giant tortoises in the Galápagos, five are located on Albemarle Island. **(Right)** is the 'Cowley Mountain tortoise'. The attendant scientist gives an idea of the animal's size.*

Distinctive-looking Hood Island race, only rediscovered in 1963. Ten more adults were found in the next eight years—and these are probably the only adults that remain. More young ones, however, have been bred at the Darwin Station, for eventual return to the island.

proved successful; by December 1970 it was possible to return the first batch of twenty young tortoises to their native island. A check on these the following year showed that they were doing well and that evidently there had been no difficulty in effecting their transition from a soft upbringing on the station to the more rugged life on Duncan.

In 1969 a major step was taken with the building of a special tortoise rearing center. This meant the provision of more adequate incubators and rearing pens, and it was made possible by a grant from the Zoological Society of San Diego. The building, unique in many ways, was designed to meet the needs both of the young tortoises and those of conservation education. It now houses the young of six races: from Chatham, Indefatigable, Duncan, James, Hood, and Volcán Cerro Azul on Albemarle. Every month many hundreds of visitors pass through the station and are able not only to see the results of this work, but to learn more about the importance of and reasons for protection programs.

Also on the Darwin Station, set among the cactus forest, are the huge breeding enclosures where the adult tortoises are kept free from all disturbance during the egg-laying months from June to September. Careful precautions have been taken to ensure that there can be no possibility of the intermingling and hybridization of races. Today, this work of hatching and rearing tortoises continues under the supervision of the Park Service.

The latest bulletin from the station reports the return of a further fifty-two young Duncan tortoises to their native island. In addition, a score of Hood hatchlings are in pens, and a further forty-two eggs are in incubators. Although, of course, a great deal remains to be done, and vigilance has to be maintained at all times, the first hurdle has been crossed on this long road to recovery. Of the ten races of Galápagos tortoise under surveillance (those of Abingdon and Narborough remain enigmatic) none is now considered to be in any immediate danger of extinction.

107

INSECTS AND PLANTS

The Butterfly Trade

Protecting the Redwoods

Endangered Plants

John Burton

The Butterfly Trade

Conserve insects? Most people's reaction to such a suggestion would be something like 'you must be kidding!' But there is one group of insects which has received wide popular support for their conservation—the butterflies. The reason, no doubt, is their colorful beauty. In North America, Britain, and on the continent of Europe, nature reserves have been created for butterflies, often with elaborate management programs to ensure the survival of the right kind of habitat. In some countries the collecting of rare species—such as the birdwings (*Ornithoptera*) of New Guinea—is banned, for it now generally recognized that the over-eager collectors have a significant effect on a butterfly population that is only just holding its own.

The same riot of color which probably stimulates the interests of many a young naturalist is also the butterfly's undoing. Many people with little or no interest in the serious study of entomology find them attractive enough to display about the home—either in museum-type cases, or flattened and embedded in objects such as coasters, ash trays, waste-paper baskets, paper weights, tray cloths and a whole host of similar objects. The use of butterfles in this way is becoming increasingly popular, particularly in North America, Europe and Japan. The butterflies used are usually exotic species from the tropics, which are often even more spectacular and beautiful than those found in the temperate regions. Butterfly 'farms' are springing up at a fantastic rate; many of them do, in fact, breed the insects destined to be speared, and adorn someone's wall, but many of the so-called farms are mainly concerned in the trade in imported species.

The butterflies imported can be roughly divided into two groups: those intended for serious collectors and those intended for purely ornamental purposes. But even to serious collectors the scientific value of the specimen is not always the most important criterion—the large and brightly colored species, such as the Papilios and Ornithopterans, almost invariably command higher prices. Rarities are sought after avidly, regardless of the possible effect on a population. A glance at one of the collectors' journals such as *The Entomologist's Record*, will show that it is quite possible to buy practically any butterfly, however rare, at a price. Fortunately, however, this type of collector is rather rare nowadays, and most entomologists today are also conservationists. It is unlikely that, for most species, the trapping of butterflies for scientific purposes has any significant effect on the overall populations.

Undoubtedly, the biggest single factor in the decline of butterflies, particularly in the densely populated regions of tropical Asia, is the destruction of the habitat—notably rainforest. But extensive collecting coupled with habitat destruction can, and often does, have a disastrous effect. The trade in ornamental butterflies, most of which originate in the Far East and South-East Asia, has increased dramatically over the past few years. Both

Brook's birdwing, from Malaysia. These large and colorful butterflies are widely exploited.

the old-established entomological dealers and the more recently established and rapidly expanding butterfly farms, are now catering for a much wider market by selling individually-mounted specimens, boxes of pretty species, and the trinkets mentioned earlier. But even more disturbing is the fact that butterflies are even being sold in hardware shops and supermarkets. I recently came across a coaster with *Ixias pyrene*, an orange-tip from the Orient, squashed between two plates of glass which form the base. The same store also sold packets of mixed butterflies—at about the same price as mixed packets of stamps. It is this type of trade which is really disturbing to conservationists—the mass export and import for purely ornamental purposes. In June 1972 a British firm, Sekers Fabrics Ltd, advertised a display of 'Unique designs of butterfly tables and wall montages. Modern adonized aluminium tables lined with Sekers Fabrics and embellished with butterflies'. This frivolous use of animals needs to be stopped before it becomes a real craze; there is always the serious danger that should such objects become popular then there is always bound to be someone who wants rarities.

The exact effects of the trade are very difficult to determine. In most countries there is virtually no control over the importation of dried insect specimens, however rare they are, in any quantity, regardless of the fact that they may have been smuggled illegally from their country of origin. Records of the numbers involved are difficult to obtain but entomologists visiting the Far East, and Taiwan in particular, have remarked on the apparent decline in the numbers of the butterflies involved in the large-scale trapping operations, though in most cases they are still fairly abundant. An idea of the scale of operations can be gained from the fact that in 1969 the industriousness of the inhabitants of Taiwan was widely praised—they apparently earn about $30 million (£12 million) a year from the sale of butterflies.

In Britain, butterflies such as the *Ixias* and *Eurema*

All the attractive species, like the newly emerged Malayan butterfly are under pressure from collectors. But though the trade has expanded dramatically in recent years, a greater threat is habitat destruction. However, add the two together and the effect can be disastrous.

species sell for as little as 65 cents (25p) when mounted in coasters and ash trays; the giant wood-nymph (*Idea leuconoe*) with a wing-span of 13 cms, sells for only $1.25 (50p). In order to make an export order of $30 million the numbers must obviously be vast—the actual collector will only be given a few cents for each specimen, and so he will need to trap large numbers. In the case of the larger and rarer species a higher price is commanded —the most ever paid for a butterfly was for the birdwing *Ornithoptera allottei*, which fetched $1,875 (£750) at auction in Paris; not only is it a beautiful species but it is also rare.

Although some species of birdwings have been bred in captivity most of them are trapped. This trapping creates a problem for conservationists—just how harmful is it? Most of the specimens trapped are males, the females tending to live higher in the forest canopy. So it is possible that trapping the males has no significant effect on the populations; but it is also possible that the females need several matings, but since so little is known about the biology of these (and many other) butterflies, it would be better not to prejudice their survival by uncontrolled collecting. The Solomon Islands are losing much of their habitat. *Ornithoptera victoria* may be common now, but will it be able to stand the threat of habitat destruction *and* collecting? All the rarer species of birdwings are protected in the Solomons, but it is quite legal to trade in them elsewhere, there is always going to be incentive for poaching.

Most of the countries which supply the world's market with butterflies are unable effectively to enforce any protection measures, even should they exist—protection therefore needs to come at the receiving end. If entomologists and collectors want to continue to be able to buy specimens from dealers, then they must help the conservationists with the factual evidence that is needed. At present a volume on butterflies in the *Red Data Book* series has yet to be published; there are few facts on the effects of commercial collecting in South-East Asia—or practically any other tropical region.

Who is engaged in the trade? How many butterflies are involved? What species are threatened? These and many other questions remain to be answered. The entomological journals, and even the conservation journals, are sadly lacking in information, and yet the much-needed information must be somewhere—perhaps tucked away in a notebook. The ardent collector will argue that butterflies, like most insects, can build up their populations fantastically rapidly, from just a few individuals. But until we know more about their population dynamics and general biology it is surely safer to control what must be one of the most frivolous and pointless trades involving live animals.

Though butterflies are sold to serious collectors, it is the mass trade for ornamental purposes that is giving cause for concern. Here are two frivolous uses of butterflies —as coasters, and for decoration of a tray-cloth.

John V. Smyth

Protecting the Redwoods

Many animal species have been reprieved from imminent extinction because people feel sentimental about them: others, unfortunately, find few champions because they are 'ugly' by our conventional standards. A leopard, perhaps, or a graceful antelope has a better chance of being conserved than a creature like a crocodile or a snake. As with animals, so it is with plants—with the difference that we find it hard to believe that *any* plant could become extinct . . . there seem to be so many of them.

But, of course, very many plants are threatened by man's activities in one way or another. And some of the world's most spectacular plants, the redwoods of California, are as threatened as any. While certainly not in danger of becoming extinct, the great redwood trees face one big problem: they have a tremendous economic value. The lumbermen covet them mightily. The famous John Muir recognized this back in the last century. 'No doubt these trees would make good lumber after passing through a sawmill,' he remarked acidly, 'as George Washington after passing through the hands of a French cook would have made good food.'

Well, they have made good lumber, and to the despair of conservationists, continue to do so. However, they are also being conserved. The fight to establish the Redwood National Park, some 300 miles north of San Francisco, ended in October 1968 after a bitter five-year battle. The private owners of this valuable timber were reluctant to surrender it to the National Park Service; they and many residents of northern California (dependent on the timber companies for jobs) are prepared to continue to fight against any further enlargement of the park, though this is what is required in the opinion of conservationists.

The fact is that the new Redwood National Park was created out of a series of compromises. Everyone had a

Gold Beach.

Redwood National Park, California, was created in 1968 after a tremendous struggle. It was the most expensive national park ever, but even now is thought to be too small.

So-called immortal tree has survived lightning, forest fire, the logger's axe, and a flood. As the sign says, it is 248 feet tall, and contains enough timber to build several homes.

*Death of the giants: scenes at a redwood lumber mill at Fort Bragg, California (**top and below right**). The buzz of the sawmills can be heard from almost any place in Redwood National Park, so small is it. But at least it does give protection to the giant trees. The photograph (**below left**) was taken near but outside the park — and shows what happens to redwoods when men build freeways.*

say during those five years—not only conservationists and lumbermen, but government departments, legislators at every level, and President Johnson and California Governor Ronald Reagan. The result was the most expensive national park ever created—at $92 million (£43 million)—and an outline that resembles a jigsaw puzzle. Consisting of some six blocks fitted in amongst blocks of private and other public land, the park is only about forty-six miles long from north to south, while it is less than ten miles wide at its greatest. The law that Lyndon Johnson signed in 1968 provided for a total park area of 58,000 acres. Of this, only 30,500 acres was acquired from private ownership, and received protection for the first time. The remaining 27,500 acres of the designated area was already protected by the State of California, and comprised the three state parks of Prairie Creek, Del Norte Coast, and Jedediah Smith.

The law did not force these to be handed over to the National Park Service by the State of California. It only said they would come under federal administration if California donated them. This California has not so far done. In fact, while it would probably be better to have the whole area under Park Service control, because it would then benefit from an overall management plan, it is also argued that if California does not donate this land (which it has protected pretty well over the years) then Washington would have to look elsewhere for a further 27,500 acres to make up the full acreage agreed by Congress. But is this really about to happen? The fund for buying land for national parks is not too flush with money, and there are plenty of people who regard parks as a fairly low priority item.

Not only is the Redwood National Park too small, (you can easily hear the surrounding sawmills from virtually anywhere in the park), in several places it is actually threatened by the timber companies' clear-cutting operations in their adjacent territory. Clear-cutting really means just what it suggests: everything goes, trees, undergrowth, even the soil is upturned. The trouble is that this part of California is also quite unstable, and landslides and erosion—though natural processes—are much more likely if the trees are clear-cut. And redwood trees are particularly susceptible to soil erosion, having shallow root systems.

I said earlier that the redwoods are in no danger of extinction. There are some one and a half million acres of redwoods left today, about 80 per cent of the area that ever was covered with them. But the question must be asked—is a redwood really a redwood while it is still immature? The quintessential redwood, surely, is a massive giant, older than any man, older than America, and towering 300 feet or more. And right now only some 150,000 acres (perhaps only 100,000 acres) of these trees are as much as a hundred years old—significantly, the age at which lumbermen like them best.

Incidentally, it is often claimed that the redwoods are the largest of all living things, with the tallest measured at 367.8 feet. But a Douglas fir which was felled in British Columbia, Canada, in 1940 measured 417 feet—and experienced loggers claimed at the time that even larger ones had been felled and were still standing. The Australian Government has cited a mountain gum tree of 382 feet. As to age—another redwood specialty—they are usually thought to live to some 3,000 to 3,500 years old; but here again they do not hold the record, for the bristlecone firs of California's White Mountains have been put at over 4,000 years—and another Australian tree, a cycad, has been estimated at 12,000 years of age. These ages are almost impossibly old for us humans to comprehend: 3,500 years places their birth more or less in the reign of the Egyptian Tutankhamen—or before the Exodus led by Moses—while 12,000 years is back in the last ice age. But if the redwood is not the world-record holder, it is a truly magnificent tree, and eminently deserving of conservation in its virgin state.

Dwarfing the human figures at its base, this great tree towers hundreds of feet high. Such giants are tempting to lumbermen, who fight further enlargement of the park—as do local residents, for whom logging operations mean jobs.

Jon Tinker

Endangered Plants

Once destroyed, a plant or animal is gone for ever. Dead as the dodo is rightly a proverb of implacable finality. We hear much of the mammals and birds which are currently endangered. Many people nowadays would accept that man has an ethical obligation to save the white rhino, the giant panda or the Arabian oryx. It would surely be equally wrong to let our 20,000 endangered wild flowers vanish from the earth.

In a materialistic world, appeals to morality tend to fall on deaf ears. What makes our neglect of wildlife the more extraordinary, for plants even more than for animals, is that we need to conserve them for reasons of unarguable practicality which ought to satisfy the most blinkered and self-centered among us. A widespread if unspoken myth of technological civilization is that everything new and worthwhile comes out of a factory or a laboratory. The sophisticated city-dweller may laugh at the child who thought milk came from bottles and not cows, but on most subjects he is just as ignorant. Some drugs are indeed invented in the lab, but far more are found ready-made in plants. Some of our furniture may be made from plastic, but most of it is based on timbers, many of which were commercially unknown only a few decades ago.

There is a curious belief that man has already exploited all of nature's products which are worth having —one of the many backward-looking and unimaginative views of a society dominated by engineers and economists. Is it not absurd to imagine that the score or so of major food plants which we use today are all that mankind will ever need? That sheep, pigs and cows are the best possible sources of meat? That agriculture can only develop by improving the species of animal and plant which were already domesticated in our great grandfathers' time? It is certain that we will increasingly have to search nature for new vegetables, new domestic animals and new fodder plants to feed them on, new medicines, new timbers and fibers, new flowers for our gardens and new scents for our pleasure. Man's most precious raw material is not iron or copper or titanium, but the vast wealth of animal and plant species which are scattered across his planet.

We cannot say that any particular flower or tree will one day provide us with a new drug or a fresh crop. But it is a matter of statistical certainty that among 20,000 plants there must be hundreds which will prove of direct benefit to man. To allow these species to drift inexorably into the botanical history books is to throw away possible cures for cancer, to abandon potential crops which might one day rescue millions from starvation.

Yet the astonishing situation is that almost no attention is being devoted to wild flower conservation anywhere in the world. Even the World Wildlife Fund, which has raised over $9 million (£3.5 million) internationally, has spent only a few thousand of it on plants. We do not even know the names of more than a few hundred of the 20,000 endangered species. That we have any information at all is largely due to Dr Ronald Melville, a retired professional botanist who is paid a small fee to compile the *Red Data Book* for flowers.

Red is for danger, and Dr Melville lists those plant species which are threatened: their names and description, their present and past distribution, why they have declined, their potential value to man, what steps should be taken to save them. Working in the herbarium at Kew Gardens, near London, England he has probably better facilities than could be found anywhere else in the world. One day he told me how long the task was taking him. 'Yesterday evening I sat down and wrote up one species. It had only recently been discovered and there was only one reference to it. It only took me an hour and a half, and that is very rare. For other plants I may spend three days just looking through the literature.' At the optimistic rate of one species a day it would take Ronald Melville eighty years to finish all 20,000.

His completed sheets, one per species, are published from Switzerland by the International Union for Conservation of Nature. The first sixty-eight came out in loose-leaf form in 1970, and a second batch will be published shortly. But why is progress so painfully slow? I asked Peter Scott, chairman of IUCN's Survival Service Commission, which has already published complete *Red Data Books* for mammals and birds. 'The problem is money. That's all there is to it,' Scott said. 'There ought to be at least six more people working on it, but we can't get the money because nobody seems to be interested.'

The flowers which Dr Melville describes in the first 68 sheets of his *Red Data Book* are far from uninteresting. My favourite is the Phillip Island glory pea (*Strebblorhiza speciosa*), extinct on its native volcanic islet in the Pacific, a thousand miles east of Sydney. Its profuse, rose-pink blossoms must have been seen by Captain Cook when he discovered nearby Norfolk Island in 1774, and by the petty thieves and poachers who were transported there soon afterwards to establish English sovereignty. The descendants of the Bounty mutineers and their Tahitian wives were settled on Norfolk in 1856, and like the convicts they released domestic livestock into the square mile of forest which was Phillip Island. Goats, pigs, and rabbits made short work of the vegetation, and soon the glory pea was gone.

Another *Red Data Book* pea is the jade vine (*Strongylodon macrobotrys*). Its magnificent blue-green blossoms hang down a yard long in the humid Philippine rainforest on Luzon and Mindoro. Sadly depleted by timber-cutting and by clearing for agriculture, the jade vine needs preserving if only as a superb plant for tropical gardens: nothing can compete with its flowering season from March until June. It might have another, more directly economic use: the seeds of a closely related species are eaten as food on nearby Guam.

A British and European entry is an orchid: the exotic and beautiful lady's slipper (*Cypripedium calcelus*). Its

Rare South
African succulent
Aloe vossii, *suffers
the depredations
of collectors.*

maroon-and-yellow flower is threatened right across Europe by picking and uprooting—the latter being a particularly silly pastime since orchids almost never transplant successfully into the garden. Fortunately, the lady's slipper is protected on one of the very few sites in Britain where it still occurs: a Yorkshire Naturalists' Trust reserve. Orchids are not the easiest of flowers to grow, but many other endangered species would probably flourish in the garden. The Calabrian primrose (*Primula palinuri*), restricted to two areas of southern Italy where it is heavily grazed and picked, is a fragrant flower whose cowslip-like scent alone makes it worth saving. Another huge horticultural group is the heathers: all but fifteen of the 630 species come from South Africa, and many are already established garden favorites. The Juno heath (*Erica junonia*) grows above the winter snow-line 6,000 feet up in the Hex River Mountains and is so rare that it has only been collected by botanists on four occasions. The jasmine heather (*Erica jasminiflora*) is restricted to a single population near Caledon in the Cape, where its habitat has been partly plowed up for wheat and bulldozed away for a new highway.

Paradoxically, while many of the endangered heathers are threatened by burning, the seeds of blushing bride (*Serruria florida*) seem to germinate better after a bush fire. Although it is now established in California and Australia as well as in South Africa, where it was once used for wedding bouquets, blushing bride is limited in the wild to a few plants in the same place near Paarl, where it was first spotted in 1780.

Goats, to the botanist the most pernicious creatures on earth, are largely responsible for the destruction of the flora of St Helena. When the island was discovered in 1502 the St Helena redwood (*Trochetia erythroxylon*) grew twenty feet tall on the rich volcanic soils among cabbage trees and giant ferns. Fifty years later a visitor recorded a herd of introduced goats a mile long—rather a lot for an island only ten miles across. Those redwoods which remained in the barren, eroded landscape were chopped down by the European settlers for firewood. Today, only one redwood grows on St Helena, although there is a chance some exist in cultivation around the Mediterranean.

Many of Ronald Melville's first sixty-eight candidates for extinction are attractive plants of value to the gardener. But their potential uses do not stop there. Ford's tree of heaven (*Ailanthus fordii*), known only from twenty specimens in Hong Kong, is closely related to the so-called Brooklyn tree (*A. altissima*), which braves smog, poor soil, leg-lifting dogs, and clambering children to provide foliage for New York. Ford's tree of heaven might prove able to brighten up other drab cities—if it survives.

It is, of course, impossible to argue that any one of the threatened plants would definitely prove useful to man. But there is no such doubt when one talks of 20,000. Many people will feel that the loss of a tenth of the

planet's flora, while perhaps regrettable, still leaves 90 per cent of our flowers: surely enough for all practical purposes. This ignores the central technique which plant breeders use to increase yields of food, drugs, or other products. Digitalin, one of the staple drugs for treatment of heart disease, used to be extracted from the English foxglove. The margin between effective and toxic doses was narrow: if you took a little too much, you might have died. Now the very similar drug digoxin is obtained from the Spanish foxglove. Its safety margin is far larger, and the doctor has a safer tool. Like a detective, the drug-searcher always questions the close relatives of a suspect. But the detective, unlike the druggist, makes sure the relatives haven't disappeared when they're needed.

Improving a food-plant usually involves cross-breeding between many different strains, races, and species. Primitive wheat, first used perhaps 10,000 years ago in Mesopotamia, was even then a cross between at least three different species of wild grass, and its ancestry has become far more complex since. Considering the extent to which wild flower conservation has been neglected, even by botanists themselves, one might think that the

Phillip Island, a thousand miles east of Sydney in the Pacific Ocean, was once completely forested but has now been denuded by rabbits, goats, and pigs. The two trees **(below left)** *are the only two specimens of the Norfolk Island pine which still grow on Phillip Island. The black cabbage tree* **(below)** *is one of about three which still remain on St Helena: goats have almost completely destroyed the thick forest*

search for new and exploitable plants belonged in the theoretical future. Far from it. Only last year the World Health Organization recorded the discovery of what may prove to be a powerful tool against a debilitating disease which is rife acro s much of Africa. Bilharzia is caused by a parasitic fluke, whose lifecycle takes place partly in human blood vessels and partly inside water snails. In Ethiopia there is a plant called soapberry (*Phytolacca dodecandra*), whose dried berries are used for washing clothes. Downstream of communal washing places there are virtually no snails, and careful research has demonstrated that soapberries contain a powerful snail-killing compound, lethal to bilharzia-carrying species.

Many wild plants contain drugs which have been used in folk medicine for generations, and some of the great chemical companies every year spend considerable sums investigating them. When in 1949 cortisone was found to cause dramatic improvements in rheumatoid arthritis, the US Government set up a worldwide search for plants containing compounds which could easily be converted to cortisone in the laboratory. For fifteen years sisals, aloes, yuccas, and yams from every corner of the globe were tested for cortisone-precursors. Another American plant-

hunt was mounted for alkaloids to treat heart disease, and in 1952 reserpine from the Indian snakeroot *Rauvolfia serpentina* was discovered to lower blood pressure as well as to tranquillize schizophrenics. A third US screening program is currently under way for tumor-suppressive compounds which might provide a treatment for cancer: the rosy periwinkle (*Catharanthus roseus*) from Jamaica, which contains over fifty alkaloids, provides two drugs which are already on the market.

America is not the only country to have searched its own and other people's flowers for new medicaments. Following the shortage of imported synthetic drugs during World War Two, the Australian Phytochemical Survey discovered over 200 indigenous alkaloidal species, among them sources for hyoscine (a muscle relaxant) and atropine (which dilates the pupil of the eye). Some countries have concentrated on particular families already known to be rich in alkaloids: Canada studied poppies, New Zealand looked at peas, Russia examined buttercups, Japan hunted for magnolias. Yet in spite of all this scrutiny, only two per cent of our known wild flower species have so far been investigated for alkaloids. Judging by the results, there may be another 50,000 potential new drugs hidden inside flowers, seeds, leaves, and roots.

So far, agricultural research has centred on making existing food crops grow where conditions for them are less suitable. In future, we may expect to see attention focused on native species which already grow luxuriantly, and then searching for ways of making them edible.

No one knows how many wild flowers become extinct every year: my guess would be somewhere between 50 and 200 species. What can be done to stem this relentless attrition? While captive breeding in zoos can provide a last resort for animals, botanic gardens are less satisfactory for plants. For one thing, similar species which do not grow side by side in nature will, planted next to one another in a garden, almost certainly interbreed. For another, the value of a plant to the breeder is its genetic make-up, and cultivated plants are often propagated by cutting or grafts. A species may grow in botanic gardens all over the world, yet genetically consist of hundreds of identical twins. Fortunately, botanists are beginning to talk of new techniques for preserving rare flowers, storing the seed under ideal conditions and growing plants only once every few decades.

Before we can plan a strategy for conservation, we need to take stock. Which species are threatened, where do they still occur, and how can they best be safeguarded? The task of indexing the endangered 20,000 in the *Red Data Book* has been started at Kew. To provide another six people, as Peter Scott suggests, would pay immense conservation dividends within a year and enable the task to be completed in a decade. The annual cost might be $50,000 (£20,000) a year. Not much, one might think, for the food and drug industries, whose combined research budgets must total hundreds of millions of dollars.

The rare South African flower Protea grandiceps **(below right)** *grows naturally at the summit of Table Mountain, while another Phillip Island species, the beautiful endemic shrub* Hibiscus insularis **(below)** *is one of the very few specimens that still exist there. The rare species of red hot poker* **(bottom left)** *in Natal, South Africa, is threatened by a housing project.*

7

SAVING THE HABITATS

It has long been recognized by conservationists that ultimately all attempts to save individual species of animals and plants are doomed to failure unless their habitats, or biotopes, are saved as well. One of the most striking examples of this is the national parks movement, begun in the United States with the establishment of Yellowstone a hundred years ago (and featured in detail elsewhere in this book). There is of course much that can be done to save particular species that does not involve their habitats—for example, poaching can be controlled, hunting laws passed, captive breeding programs initiated —but in the end, these wild species have to have living space to survive.

And so national parks, nature reserves, game sanctuaries, and so forth have been created in many countries.

As the world fills up with human beings, and human progress affects the remotest parts of our world, there are some key habitats which are under special pressure or which need particular vigilance to conserve them. These include wetlands, lowland tropical rainforests, cloud forests, oceanic islands, coastal and estuarine zones, circumpolar regions, desert and semi-desert areas, and high mountains. The threats are various, and include pollution, drainage, lumbering, construction, highway building, and other development.

Apart from direct financial aid, habitats can be saved by intervention by conservation organizations at the highest levels. Nevertheless, the financial aspect is crucial, for it is often necessary to acquire land urgently to hold off development while long-term measures are worked out in association with governments and local interests.

Our world map is not intended to be comprehensive; indeed, the number of areas already enjoying some measure of protection could be multiplied many times over—and the areas still in need of conservation could probably be multiplied by several thousand. Its purpose is to give a simple, selective idea of a few of the places which are now being protected, and also those most in need of protection.

The Camargue

Lake Nakuru

Yellowstone's Centenary

ARCTIC OCEAN
SOUTHERN OCEAN
Spitzbergen
Skaftafell, Iceland
Marchauen, Austria
Azraq Oasis, Jordan
Lal Suhanra, Pakistan
Caerlaverock, Scotland
Ouse Washes, England
ulness, gland
Camargue, France
Simien National Park, Ethiopia
Chitawan, Nepal
Kaziranga, India
o Donana, Spain
Sundarbans, Bangladesh/India
hegada Island
Borivali, India
Sinharaja Forest, Ceylon
ai Forest, Ivory Coast
Uda Walawe, Ceylon
Mindanao Island Philippines
Murchison Falls National Park, Uganda
Somalia
Gunung Loeser, Sumatra
Etosha Pan, S.W. Africa
Papua & New Guinea
East Zaïre / Rwanda
Seychelles
Udjung Kulon, Java
il (near Rio)
Lake Nakuru, Kenya
Nossi Mangabe, Madagascar
Malindi, Kenya
Madagascar
Ayers Rock, Alice Springs
Europa Island

Christopher Savage

Camargue

Mention the word 'wetlands' to a conservationist and he will soon list a catalog of drainage schemes threatening the wildlife of lakes, marshes, and river estuaries in many continents. Mention the same word to someone less addicted to the outdoor life, and he will think of damp windy places, usually uncomfortably hot or cold.

Wetlands are in fact among the most valuable and threatened habitats in the world—valuable to millions of wild creatures who have evolved so that they can live only in the highly specialized zones of tidal estuaries or shallow inland lakes, and valuable to man as great natural laboratories whether tidal or in the middle of a continent.

Wetlands are too often considered as mere wastelands, and their development is seen only in terms of intensive industrial or agricultural use, preceded by infilling with garbage and a rash of drainage schemes, and frequently followed by pollution or problems arising from the heavy use of fertilizers. Inevitably, as all this is going on, wildlife suffers or is often swept away altogether.

Some wetlands may be of less obvious interest or value than others (even though many kinds of wildlife find them vital). But the Camargue, an area of lagoons and marshes in the Rhône Delta of southern France, must have an immediate appeal for both scientist and tourist. The word itself spells instant romance for many people, who visualize an Eden where nature has remained untrammeled, where clouds of pink flamingos color the sky, black bulls display an awe-inspiring ferocity, and wild white horses race with streaming manes and tails through the lagoons. Sixty-five miles of golden sand stretch alongside the almost tideless Mediterranean, small white houses dot the flat landscape, while fish leap out of the dikes on a summer evening. If you should hap-

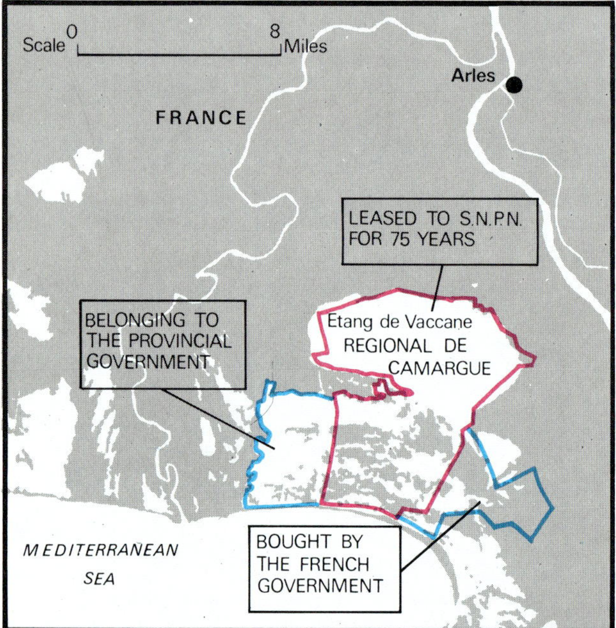

The marshes of
the Camargue are
now safe thanks
to public and
Government
co-operation.

The lithe Camargue horses *(above)* are born black, change to light gray by their fourth year, finally becoming white as adults. The asphodel's flowers *(center left)* are commonly used to decorate graves in southern Europe. The mantid *(left)* is closely related to the praying mantis.

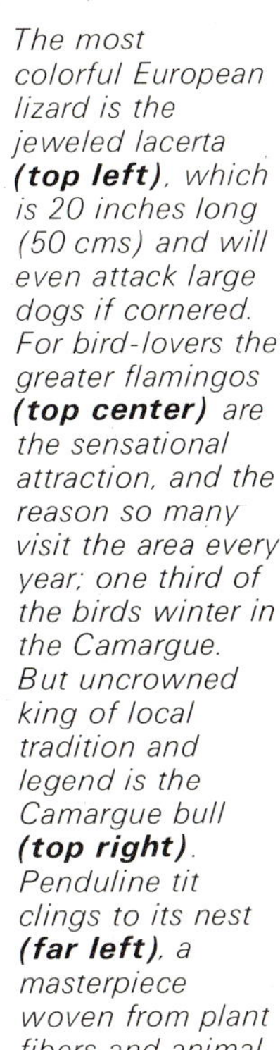

The most colorful European lizard is the jeweled lacerta (top left), which is 20 inches long (50 cms) and will even attack large dogs if cornered. For bird-lovers the greater flamingos (top center) are the sensational attraction, and the reason so many visit the area every year; one third of the birds winter in the Camargue. But uncrowned king of local tradition and legend is the Camargue bull (top right). Penduline tit clings to its nest (far left), a masterpiece woven from plant fibers and animal wool.

pen to like hoopoes and orphean warblers there will be endless interest and excitement. You can with little difficulty move away from the crowds and be alone all day amongst the lagoons, rushes, and tamarisk trees.

The Rhône rises among the snows of Switzerland and spills south towards the Mediterranean, leaving its boulders and pebbles along the way. On the last stage of its journey it divides into two distinct arms above Arles-en-Provence; these arms enclose the Camargue and fan out either side of the area, to the sea. And the sea itself infiltrates the area, sometimes gently, sometimes more forcibly when a strong south-easterly wind blows. Dikes built against the waywardness of the Rhône or the strength of the sea impose a man-made structure on the natural one, making it doubly complex.

The salinity of the water is probably the most important factor influencing the human beings and wildlife that live in the Camargue. It restricts man's use of the otherwise rich soil, but varying as it does in concentration, it provides an infinite variety of habitats for mammals, birds, and aquatic and plant life.

Parts of the Camargue have been cultivated since the sixteenth century, when it was known as the granary of Provence, and the production of wheat, rice, grapes and other fruit has intensified around the perimeter of the warm lagoons, dunes, and salt steppes. The extraction of salt, too, has increased in the south-east of the region where the salt pans stretch away in white wastes. Oil

refineries and a huge industrial complex are being built between the Camargue and Marseilles, and on a clear day Concorde can be seen taking off from Toulouse.

This multiplicity of threats may sound horrific, but the Rhône capriciously changing its course, the sea swept inland by a fierce wind, a particularly hard winter, or an especially dry summer—all these affect the wildlife of the Camargue almost as much as the human influences. The area continues to evolve ecologically; it is naturally dynamic, and the removal of the salt extractors or the power cables would not alter its essentially shifting character.

While some species of birds have decreased in number with the more intensive use of the land—for example, the pratincole, the lapwing, and the great gray shrike—many can make use of it—such as the squacco and night herons, the black-tailed godwit, and the wood sandpiper. Other birds are attracted to the area and flourish because of the orchards, improved pastures, and rice fields. However, the human threats are there and could become more severe. One such is the drainage of the rice fields which causes the water level to rise unexpectedly in the lakes and marshes.

At present it is too expensive to put any more land under commercial crops, and landowners have agreed with nature protection societies not to develop the salt steppes or drain the marshes. The day may come, however, when it could become profitable to grow more olive trees, or to plant more fields with lucerne. And at that time more barbed wire fences will enclose the habitats of more wild species. Even more likely, there will be an increasing incentive to extend the salt pans, which although they attract some species at certain times of the year, are completely devoid of mammals and birds for long periods.

But the Camargue is not a free-for-all for the developers. As early as 1928, a private body, the Société Nationale de Protection de la Nature, foresaw the problems and pressures to come and established part of the Camargue as a nature reserve. Les Imperieux is another nature reserve protecting some of the most valuable habitats, and is administered by the commune of Les Saintes Maries de la Mer, the small town in the Delta.

Finally, at the end of 1971, the World Wildlife Fund with a donation of one million francs ($190,000 or £75,000) co-operated with the French Government in buying large areas of the Camargue which will be added to the existing protected areas. The salt company, Cie des Salins du Midi, also co-operated by yielding some of its land in return for areas elsewhere that are less important for wildlife.

Under a new arrangement, Government, local communities, land-owners, hunters, and conservation bodies will all contribute towards the management of the new reserve areas. This co-operation and interest in a common goal—the survival of the Camargue—should ensure its safe future.

Drs M. F. I. J. Bijleveld

Lake Nakuru

The future of Kenya's Lake Nakuru, home of millions of flamingoes, is in jeopardy. This vast soda lake just south of the Equator is visited by thousands of people every year; none of them would disagree with Roger Tory Peterson who has described the great flocks of lesser flamingoes as 'the greatest ornithological spectacle in the world'.

Yet the familiar pressures of the twentieth century have finally reached this famous lake lying high in Africa's Great Rift Valley. Land shortage, population pressures, and expansion of the town of Nakuru to the edge of the lake, threaten the existence, not only of the spectacular birds but also of the habitats and game surrounding the lake.

In 1968 Lake Nakuru became the first National Park created in Africa to conserve birdlife. The lesser flamingoes, the most numerous birds found on the lake, are attracted by the warm 'pea-soup' of the water made rich by the blue-green algae, crustaceans, and insects larvae. Lake Nakuru is the main feeding ground for this species and at times as many as one and a half million of these birds can be seen here. The greater flamingo, by far the largest of the world's five races of flamingo, is also present in large numbers, usually feeding in deeper water. It is estimated that each day the flamingoes eat as much as 180 tons of algae and return 60 tons of excrement to the water; so rich are the nutrients in the lake that the algae can reproduce themselves twice a day and so support the huge concentrations of birds.

But it is not only the flamingoes that have made Nakuru famous. Nearly 400 other species of birds have been seen either on the lake or in the wide variety of habitats that surround it. Many of the birds are migrants from other parts of Africa, and in the months of the Palearctic winter the ducks and waders arrive in tens of thousands from Europe and Asia; great flocks of pintails, teal, shovelers, wood sandpipers, and ruffs pour in seeking the warmth of the African sun.

Eleven major habitat types have been distinguished around the shores of Lake Nakuru—and only two of these are at present included in the Park boundaries. The mudflats, virgin forests, and grasslands are of vital importance to an enormous variety of mammals, birds and plant life. Spoonbills and herons, storks and ibises, fish and probe the muddy shallows for food, while terns and gulls call overhead. The bateleur eagle and the African fish eagle which fishes from the lake, are just two birds of prey seen here. Falcons and owls hunt through the surrounding bush. Hawks, like the chanting goshawk, pounce on their prey, while the African harrier hawk takes smaller birds and mice from the crannies of trees. Other birds such as rails and grebes live either on

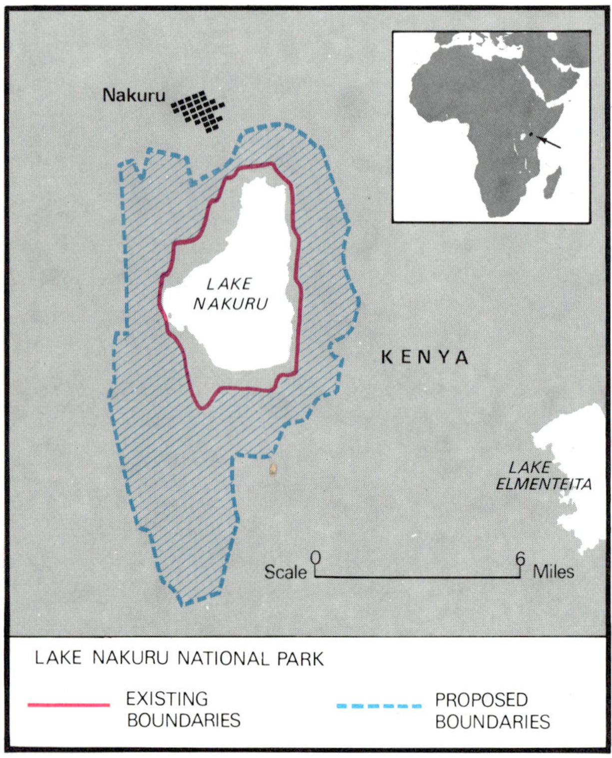

Both lesser and greater flamingoes are abundant on Lake Nakuru, though the former species is vastly more numerous (sometimes totaling as many as one and a half million). This vast soda lake—'the greatest ornithological spectacle in the world'—is in jeopardy, but conservationists are hopeful that they can save it.

the lake or near its edge. Cuckoos, kingfishers and rollers abound. A relatively new addition to the lake are the pelicans which have only recently come to Nakuru after the introduction of a small fish species found in nearby Lake Magadi.

Much of the rich mammal fauna lies outside the Park boundaries, which leaves it unprotected. Hippopotamus, rhinoceros, waterbuck and reedbuck, impala and eland are plentiful; more rarely leopards are seen. Baboons, vervet monkeys, and the black and white colobus bound or swing through much of the forest and grassland.

The wonderfully balanced eco-system of Lake Nakuru has evolved over thousands of years, and the basis of just about everything is the algae. Until recently the land around the lake remained relatively undisturbed—and in some areas it was completely untouched. As land suitable for agriculture becomes scarce, people are starting to look with longing at the virgin slopes of the surrounding hills, and at the grasslands and forests occupied now only by wildlife. Large estates are being broken up and the land, quite unsuitable for the methods of the African farmer, is nevertheless sold to him. Woodlands

are in danger of being cut down which will lead to erosion and the silting up of the lake. Fertilizers and pesticides are used liberally in an effort to increase productivity of the often stony ground, and in turn threaten the lake with pollution. The development of the town of Nakuru, and the problems of increased sewage disposal, will contribute to the deterioration of the rich food sources in the lake which has no outlet and in which pollutants will concentrate. As soon as the food supply diminishes, this natural wonder that is Lake Nakuru, will disintegrate. The millions of birds relying on it will disappear, and the neighboring land will be developed; a wide variety of trees and plants will be swept away, and the game will be driven out of the bush. A lifeless mudflat will remain, visited by no one.

UNESCO has recommended to the Kenyan Government, after an intensive study, that the Park boundaries should be extended up to a mile from the lakeshore to create an effective buffer zone. This should have the effect of halting the expansion of Nakuru town to the edge of the lake. Efforts are now being made to purchase the necessary land to create this buffer zone, and the Kenya National Parks Board, who approved the UNESCO recommendation, has asked for help of the World Wildlife Fund to raise money for land purchase. Together the Kenya National Parks and World Wildlife must raise over $300,000 (£120,000) to save the land from development.

As part of an international plan for raising money, World Wildlife has appealed to the young people of Europe, who are now conducting fund-raising campaigns in Britain, Belgium, Luxembourg, the Netherlands, Sweden and Switzerland. Help is also coming from the young people in Kenya itself. Members of the Nakuru Wildlife Club collected thousands of small flamingo feathers, which were sent to Holland in order to raise funds for the Park.

If this massive international effort fails, a great natural asset of immense scientific, educational and esthetic value will be lost forever. Since the beginning of this century 90 per cent of Kenya's wildlife and its wild places have disappeared. Eroded by small-scale farming, the forests and grasslands with their native flora and fauna have dwindled disastrously. Despite these heavy losses the government of Kenya and other African countries are fortunate that their continent, more than any other, is still associated with teeming wildlife. The airline advertisements and travel journals continue to tell the world that Africa's game still exists in abundance and that 'its wild heart remains untamed'. Such optimism will sustain a severe blow if Nakuru is lost.

The ecologically fragile wonders of Nakuru are in danger of vanishing; if they do there will be widespread dismay throughout the conservation movement, and the long-term effects on the East African tourist industry will be incalculable.

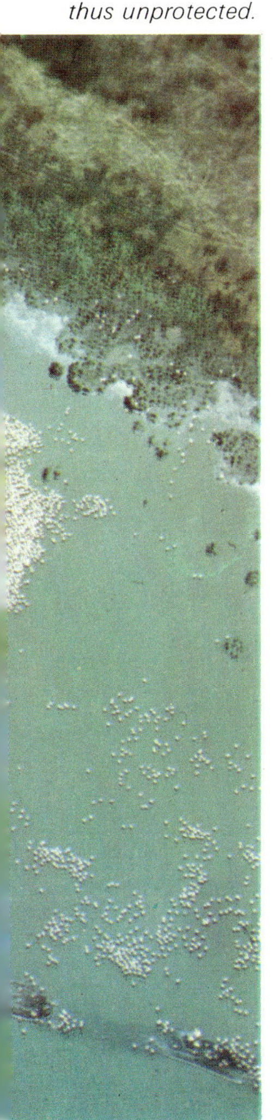

*Though flamingoes **(below right)** are the main attraction, Nakuru has much other wildlife to put on display. It can boast nearly 400 other bird species, and it has a rich mammal fauna, such as waterbuck **(bottom right)**. Many of the mammals live outside the present park boundaries, however, and are thus unprotected.*

Robert Sanders

Yellowstone Centenary

The world's first national park was established in the United States just a century ago. It was on 1 March 1872 that President Ulysses S. Grant put his signature on the law that created Yellowstone National Park—some two million acres, or 3,472 square miles to be exact—on the upper reaches of the Yellowstone River in north-western Wyoming. But it is more than a centenary that Yellowstone has celebrated: for the national park concept has probably done more to conserve wildlife than any other single endeavor. There are now more than 1,000 national parks around the world, and the phrase has come to be synonomous with conservation itself.

Various early expeditions west brought back reports

Yellowstone National Park is a tourist mecca (two million people visit its two million acres every year)—but it is still a haven for wildlife, which is relatively varied and abundant. Black bears **(left)** can cause accidents because they have lost their fear of man, through being fed by visitors, who in turn fail to remember that bears can be dangerous. Other species, like the mule deer **(left center)** tolerate human beings in the park as long as they keep their distance. Besides wildlife, Yellowstone is famed for its scenic attractions like the geysers and hot springs **(below)**, of which it has more than 10,000, and Lower Falls, on the Grand Canyon of the Yellowstone **(far left)**

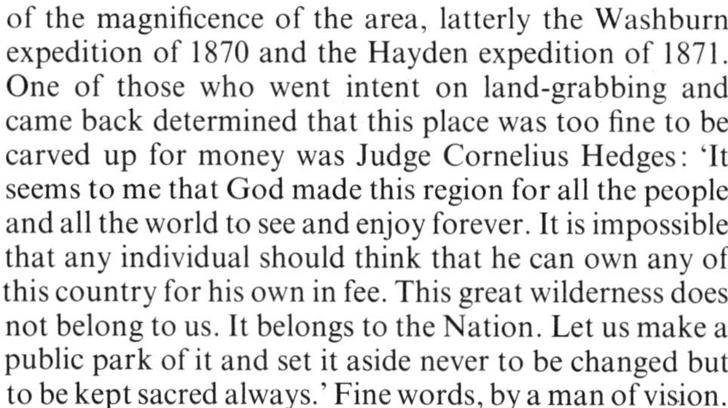

of the magnificence of the area, latterly the Washburn expedition of 1870 and the Hayden expedition of 1871. One of those who went intent on land-grabbing and came back determined that this place was too fine to be carved up for money was Judge Cornelius Hedges: 'It seems to me that God made this region for all the people and all the world to see and enjoy forever. It is impossible that any individual should think that he can own any of this country for his own in fee. This great wilderness does not belong to us. It belongs to the Nation. Let us make a public park of it and set it aside never to be changed but to be kept sacred always.' Fine words, by a man of vision.

Yellowstone was established to be a 'public park or pleasuring ground . . . for the benefit and enjoyment of all people'. It has indeed provided both of these things in its first hundred years. Still the largest American park, it covers an area larger than the State of Rhode Island. It boasts more than 10,000 geysers, hot springs, and mud volcanoes. Its scenery is breathtaking and its scope vast. Of wildlife it has variety and relative abundance: though wolves and mountain lions are now very scarce, there are thousands of elk, perhaps 600 bighorn sheep, 600 bison, 1,000 moose, and several hundred black and grizzly bears. There are also coyotes, pronghorn, many smaller mammals, and about 250 species of birds. Four-fifths of the area is forested. Some of the wildlife creates problems. The elk, for example, are too numerous and have to be culled or transported to other areas where they are not so abundant. And bears, accustomed to being fed by camera-toting tourists, have lost most of their fear of man—and in turn regularly cause accidents because tourists do not treat them with proper respect.

Yellowstone is popular, and is annually visited by upwards of two million people. This may sound a lot—and in the height of the season when cars are nose to tail on the park road system, it may seem too many. However, Yellowstone is still a wilderness for those who like wilderness. It has been estimated that the vast majority of the visitors never leave the roads, camp-sites, and other developed areas. Most of them only use 5 per cent of the park.

Despite the problems caused by its very popularity, Yellowstone is still in many ways America's (and the world's) premier national park. Its staff have a new plan for coping with the ever-increasing number of visitors, with the aim that not only will the tourists get more out of their visits, but the park's own unique wilderness values will be preserved. Its original creation started a trend in conservation, and it can still be an example to the world.

Emergency Action Summary

Today, wildlife conservation is widely accepted, at least in the developed world; and in the undeveloped or Third World it is accepted by a substantial minority, even though it may not be immediately obvious how conservation can be reconciled with the pressing demands in the poorer countries for a better quality of life.

This is a remarkably different situation to that of as little as a decade ago, when those who believed that wildlife should be conserved had to marshal every reason they could think of to justify their beliefs. Nowadays, although there are still large pockets of resistance, it is not so much a question of *why* conservation is necessary, as to *how* it can be achieved.

Nevertheless, this change in attitude has come upon the world at a critical period for wildlife. It has arrived just in time, perhaps too late for many species. Throughout this book, reference has been made to the looseleaf *Red Data Book* of the International Union for Conservation of Nature (in fact, of its Survival Service Commission). This is the basic data bank of wildlife conservation, listing as it does the wild animals and plants around the world which are in danger of extinction. As of late 1972, there were some 767 kinds of animals listed in the *Red Data Book*. Of these, 294 were mammals, 281 birds, 86 reptiles, 27 amphibians, and 79 fishes. This does not count the plants, of which about 125 have so far been listed (but which undoubtedly total many, many more), and it is doubtless low in other areas, such as the fish, due mainly to the relatively little analytical work which has been carried out.

Most work has been done on the mammals and birds, and these two totals are probably a reasonable reflection of the true situation. In 1969, James Fisher and others estimated that of the mammals and birds that had become extinct since the year 1600, about one-quarter had died out naturally. The other three-quarters had become extinct because of man's presence or activities.

Of course, not all the creatures on the endangered list are equally threatened, and the *Red Data Book* recognizes this distinction by printing some entries on special red-colored pages—for critically endangered species. There are 74 kinds of mammals and 67 different birds which rate this degree of concern. Jane Fenton has estimated that over-exploitation by man is the main cause of this situation for the mammals (about 60 per cent), while for the birds, the main cause is loss of habitat. But between them, over-exploitation and loss of habitat (both human activities) are overwhelmingly responsible for the plight facing these two groups of animals.

It appears, then, that man's influence on the survival of wildlife species is becoming more extreme, which one might have expected. Between 1600 and the present, man has been responsible for perhaps 75 per cent of the mammal and bird extinctions; but of the most seriously endangered forms at present, 87 per cent are in that plight because of man.

While the rate of extinction seems to have been held to about one kind a year this century, it seems likely that it could suddenly start to climb. We are managing to hold the line, just, but as each year goes by, more animals are becoming scarcer. As Roger Tory Peterson points out in his introduction, this book tends to concentrate on the 'glamor' species: there may be a number of less visible, less well-known creatures which are inexorably declining in number.

Certain groups of animals and plants are under particular pressure. These tend to be the ones which have the greatest economic importance for mankind—such as the whales, the seals, the spotted cats, the turtles, and the crocodilians—or which man has traditionally regarded as his enemy or competitor—such as the carnivores, the birds of prey, and (again) the crocodilians. Others are exploited because of their esthetic appeal, like the orchids, amongst the plants.

Increasingly, however, mankind is coming to realize that he stands to lose a great deal if these living things are allowed to become extinct. He stands to lose out economically, but above all scientifically. It is now recognized that we need the biological diversity that all these animals and plants represent. Our life systems on planet earth may not be able to withstand the loss of these important links in the ecological chains. It is increasingly accepted that the integrity of our biological systems must be preserved.

Though wildlife conservationists have had to devote much of their global effort to last-ditch action to save animals from final extinction, they have always tried to act in time to preserve populations before they get down to this point of no-return. And one of the best means of saving viable populations is to save whole habitats—sometimes called biotopes. Wilderness conservation is the fundamental means of preserving these ecosystems intact, and this is why conservation efforts are increasingly being directed towards saving the habitats, towards establishing new national parks, nature reserves, game sanctuaries, and stepping up the protection of existing areas. If the wilderness is adequately preserved, the animals and plants—as a community—will be preserved too.

Conservation action means, first of all, concern then action by people. But a minority enthusiasm cannot be truly successful in today's world without the co-operation of governments. And this is where the great progress has taken place in the past decade. An increasing awareness by the world's decision-makers first became publicly apparent with the conference in Strasbourg, France, to mark the start of European Conservation Year in 1970. And then in 1972 we had the first United Nations Conference on the Human Environment in Stockholm, Sweden.

By no means a total success, the Stockholm conference did achieve two things. It showed those governments who still didn't take the environment seriously that there are many others who do; and it showed the rich nations that the poor ones have got to be helped to get a greater share of the globe's riches before they can be expected to show much enthusiasm for conserving its wildlife and wild places. There was a huge gulf between the industrialized and the underdeveloped world at Stockholm, and far too much narrow nationalism; but the talking had begun, the important first step along what will prove a difficult path towards solving (or at least controlling) the world's environmental problems.

Though the agreements reached at Stockholm may only be the tentative beginnings of a new global environmental ethic, they do indicate that people, and through them governments, have at last begun to perceive the importance of conservation of nature and the environment.

And, too, it is now being recognized that the world environment cannot be handled piecemeal; there is much that is valuable—many animals and plants and wildernesses—in every corner of the world. The poor nations alone cannot be expected to solve their conservation problems unaided.

So far, considerable conservation effort has been evident in Europe and North America. Africa, too, especially East and Southern Africa, has seen a variety of conservation programs. But some parts of the world have been neglected. The World Wildlife Fund and IUCN, for example, the major international wildlife conservation bodies, over the past ten years spent just on two-thirds of their available funds in Europe and Africa combined. Only 4.6 per cent went to Asia and a scant one per cent to South America. It is planned to redress this uneven balance to a large extent.

ENDANGERED ANIMALS

Mammals	294	Amphibians	27
Birds	281	Fishes	79
Reptiles	86		

CRITICALLY ENDANGERED ANIMALS—MAIN CAUSES

Mammals

Over-exploitation	44 (60%)
Loss of habitat	24 (33%)
Not known	6 (8%)
	74 (100%)

Birds

Over-exploitation	20 (30%)
Loss of habitat	36 (54%)
Not known	11 (16%)
	67 (100%)

BELOW IS A SELECTION OF SIXTEEN OF THE MOST INTERESTING AND ENDANGERED ANIMALS.

The reasons why each needs emergency action are summarised in the following six pages.

MAMMALS

Tiger	132
Cheetah	132
Polar bear	132
Javan rhinoceros	132
European bison	132
Swamp deer	134
Golden lion marmoset	134

MARINE MAMMALS

Fin whale	134

BIRDS

Whooping crane	134
Hawaiian goose	134
Japanese crested ibis	134
Spanish imperial eagle	136
Galápagos flightless cormorant	136
Trumpeter swan	136

REPTILES

Green turtle	136

FISH

Devil's Hole pupfish	136

SPECIES		RANGE	POPULATION
INDIAN TIGER (*Panthera tigris tigris*) 	Similar to lion in size—about 450 lbs, 9 feet long. Solitary; hunts by night. Preys on a variety of mammals, from small deer to young elephants. Adults kill about thirty times a year. Normally avoids man. Two to four cubs, lives twenty-five years or more. One of 8 races of tigers.	Present distribution patchy over India, Bangladesh, Nepal, Sikkim, Bhutan, Burma. Habitat ranges through humid evergreen forests, dry open jungle, grassy swamps.	40,000 in 1930; 30,000 in 1939; currently about 2,600 —in India (2,000), Bangladesh (100), Nepal (200), Bhutan (200), a few in Sikkim and Burma.
CHEETAH (*Acinonyx jubatus*) 	Fastest four-legged animal, can reach 60 mph. Only cat with permanently extended claws. Weight 100 lbs, length $7\frac{1}{2}$ feet. Generally hunts in pairs in cooler part of day, and for medium-sized mammals. Life-span sixteen years.	Formerly widely distributed over southern Asia, from Arabia to India, and Africa south of the Sahara. Now only relict populations in western part of Asiatic range —southern Russia, Iran, Afghanistan, possibly Saudi Arabia. In Africa much reduced everywhere. Prefers open grassland or scrub.	Possibly 100-200 in Asia, more numerous in Africa, though population inside National Parks only thought to be about 2,000.
POLAR BEAR (*Thalarctos maritimus*) 	One of the largest bears, and most carnivorous. Weight about 900 lbs, height about 8 feet. Solitary animal, adults only meet to mate. Wander constantly over pack ice in search of food. Usually two young. Life-span about thirty years.	Circumpolar regions of northern hemisphere; on and off pack ice.	Significant decline since 1930s; now thought to be about 10,000–20,000.
JAVAN RHINOCEROS (*Rhinoceros sondaicus*) 	Similar appearance to Indian rhinoceros, but slightly smaller. Skin smooth (without tubercles of Indian rhino) with deep folds. Weight about 1 ton, height $5\frac{1}{2}$ feet at shoulder.	Formerly from Bengal, Burma, Thailand, Cambodia, Laos, and Vietnam into Malaya, Sumatra, and Java. Now confined to Udjung Kulon reserve on extreme western tip of Java, and possibly a small population in Loeser area of Sumatra. Preferred habitat secondary forest growth.	Estimated at twenty-two in Udjung Kulon, Java, in early 1960s; population now totals forty-two. Sumatra population unknown, but same order of magnitude, or less.
EUROPEAN BISON (*Bison bonasus*) 	Also known as wisent. Exterminated in truly wild state. Less shaggy, longer legs, greater body length, and smaller head than American bison. Good sense of smell, weak eyesight. Single young. Only small seasonal migration.	Once ranged over western and southern Europe, east to the Caucasus and north to Siberia, now reduced to mainly Bialowieza Forest in Poland and various zoos. A woodland animal, it browses on ferns, leaves, and bark.	Bialowieza herd numbered 700 in 1914, but all were slaughtered during First World War. From a captive nucleus, reintroduced herd built up again to current total of about 700-800 (including zoo specimens).

THE PROBLEM	ACTION TAKEN	ACTION NEEDED	SURVIVAL RATING POPULATION TREND
Orgy of trophy-hunting begun by British, continued by other foreigners and wealthy Indians. Present hazards: widespread poaching for valuable skin; destruction of habitat and natural prey; killing because of man-eating and 'cattle-lifting' habits (real or imagined).	Legally protected in India, Bangladesh, Nepal, Bhutan. US and Britain prohibit tiger skin imports. Campaigns in western countries discouraging use of tiger skin. Some reserves established. Preliminary population, behavior studies carried out.	Crackdown on poaching. Close black market in Indian subcontinent. Import restrictions in other consumer countries, especially Europe, Japan. Bigger and better reserves, with sufficient prey species. Translocate isolated tigers to big reserves. Continued research into population and biology.	☆☆☆ ★★★★
Hunting for sport, though probably less important threat today. Hunting and poaching for valuable skin. Destruction and disturbance of habitat. Cannot co-exist in close proximity to man, so expanding human populations in Africa a major threat.	Legally protected throughout much of Africa; many countries prohibit export of skins. US and UK have import restrictions. Fur trade in most consumer countries has agreed to voluntary ban on use of skins. IUCN/IFTF survey in progress to study status, ecology of species.	Legal protection in remaining African countries; import restrictions on skins in additional consumer countries. Continued research on population dynamics, general ecology.	☆☆☆ ★★★★
Long history of persecution, because of competition with man; for skins; and most recently for sport. Use of aircraft by sport hunters, and snowmobiles by Eskimos, a major recent threat. Greater incidence of disease due to man and domestic livestock penetrating deeper into Arctic.	Total protection throughout Soviet Union. Permits reduced in Alaska, and use of aircraft in that area now banned. New conservation measures expected soon in Greenland. Total protection in Spitzbergen for five years just announced. Protected in Newfoundland.	Polar bear experts from USSR, Norway, Denmark, Canada, US have recommended total protection for polar bears from 1973 (local people to retain traditional rights). International convention required. More data on dens and new methods of tagging needed.	☆☆☆☆ ★★★★
Demand for rhino horn (especially for supposed aphrodisiac properties) caused disastrous over-exploitation. Rapid human population growth in Java caused change in land use, leading to destruction of rhino habitat. Last small population concentrated in Udjung Kulon, so extremely vulnerable to any adverse development. Poachers still a problem.	World Wildlife helped implement action program in Udjung Kulon, comprising continuing research and habitat management (planting of saplings, clearing of scrub). Firearms and other equipment provided for game guards. Rhino population responding.	Continued management of reserve, and strict protection. Rhinos' main food now scarce—further planting should take place. Gunung Loeser, Sumatra, could prove important second reserve, but currently subject to large-scale timber extraction, illegal hunting, and agriculture, so management and increased protection needed, as in Java.	☆☆☆ ★★
Hunting pressure and forest clearance reduced numbers early in twentieth century.	Gradual rebuilding of semi-captive Bialowieza herd following near extinction in 1914. Protection continued even during Second World War. Area now carefully managed and protected.	Species should be more widely distributed as insurance against disease or catastrophe similar to 1914. Only available habitat is in Soviet Union.	☆☆☆☆ ★★

Key on page 137

SPECIES		RANGE	POPULATION
SWAMP DEER (*Cervus duvauceli*)	Also known as barasingha (southern race). Reaches 4 feet at shoulder, with antlers 40 inches long. Somewhat resembles red deer.	Formerly widespread in northern and central Indian subcontinent. Now only in parts of south-west Nepal, Uttar Pradesh, West Bengal, and Assam (northern race); and in and around Kanha National Park, Madhya Pradesh (southern race). Favors extensive marshy grassland.	Northern race reduced to 3,000–4,000, and declining; southern race down to about a hundred.
GOLDEN LION MARMOSET (*Leontideus rosalia*)	Perhaps most brightly colored of all living mammals —an intense, shimmering, golden yellow. Diurnal and extremely active. Varied diet includes insects, small vertebrates, fruits, seeds, shoots. Male takes over care of young, only surrendering them to female for feeding.	Coastal forest mainly in State of Rio de Janeiro, south-eastern Brazil. Present range covers area of only 400 square miles.	Numbers reduced drastically to below 400.
FIN WHALE (*Balaenoptera physalus*) A baleen whale; second largest of the great whales. Weight 70 tons, length 82 feet. Body light gray above, pure white below. Can remain submerged thirty minutes.		Found throughout the world's oceans.	Reduced from estimated original population (before whaling began) of 430,000 to present 'exploitable' population of 100,000. Possible total population now in region of 150,000.
WHOOPING CRANE (*Grus americana*)	North America's tallest living bird. Wingspan up to $7\frac{1}{2}$ feet. Omnivorous. Nests in marsh or muskeg; lays two eggs, usually only one young reared.	Now restricted to two areas, one winter, one summer. Breeds in Wood Buffalo National Park, near Great Slave Lake, Canada; migrates 2,000 miles to winter in Arkansas National Wildlife Refuge on Gulf Coast of Texas.	Declined from mid-nineteenth century total of 1,300–1,400 to a low of only twenty-one birds in 1920s. Slow but steady increase to present fifty-nine.
HAWAIIAN GOOSE (*Branta sandvicensis*)	Also known as ne-ne. Only wild goose resident on Hawaii Island, Hawaii. Heavily-barred, gray-brown goose with black face. Feet semi-webbed. Lays four to six cream-white eggs.	Restricted to limited areas at higher altitudes (5,000–8,000 feet) on mountains of Hawaii Island. Introduced into Haleakala Crater, Maui Island, in 1960s. Lives on old lava flows in sparsely vegetated areas.	Declined from 25,000 in late nineteenth century to about fifty in 1947. Now 500 birds, including 200 on Hawaii.
JAPANESE CRESTED IBIS (*Nipponia nippon*)	One of the rarest birds in the world.	Now confined to Sado Island and possibly Noto Peninsula, Japan. Once widespread across northern China, Manchuria, and Korea as well as Japan. Prefers old trees in extensive stands to isolated trees.	Declined steadily to eight on Sado Island during this century.

THE PROBLEM	ACTION TAKEN	ACTION NEEDED	SURVIVAL RATING POPULATION TREND
Heavy, continued poaching in most parts of its range. Habitat destroyed by man and converted to agricultural use. Southern race also threatened by competition from domestic cattle and possibly chital deer.	Both races completely protected in India. Reserves established in India and Nepal. Scientific research programs. Management of grassland at Kanha.	Expansion of sanctuary areas, strengthening of protective measures. More research into reasons for decline, especially of southern race.	Northern race ☆☆☆★★ Southern race ☆☆☆★★★★
Rapid deforestation to make way for sugar cane, coffee, banana plantations, and housing projects. Capture of live specimens for animal trade.	Protected in Brazil. Wild Animal Preservation Trust is to establish several breeding centers in US; zoos will be asked to contribute animals to breeding program.	Immediate establishment of suitable reserve in Brazil, field studies to discover best means for its conservation.	☆☆★★★★★
A depleted species, below its maximum sustainable yield level due to past intensive whaling with inadequate quota restrictions.	Whaling nations now observe closed season, closed areas, size limits. Quotas reduced to 1,950 whales in Antarctic, 650 in North Pacific for 1972–73 season.	Current quota will lead to only slow rebuilding of population; zero quota, or moratorium, would give best chance of quickest recovery.	☆☆☆☆☆★★★
Intensive hunting pressure, especially during its long annual migration. Also, has been relegated by man to extreme northern part of former breeding area.	Strict protection in both wintering and breeding areas. Energetic publicity, especially by National Audubon Society, and Press. Grain planted at winter refuge keeps birds in protected area. Captive rearing program.	Continue captive rearing program, with eventual aim of conditioning young for return to wild. Extension of winter refuge.	☆☆☆★★
Predation by man, plus competition from introduced mammals and destruction of habitat by domestic stock.	Official bird of Hawaii, fully protected. Highly successful captive breeding program at, especially, the Wildfowl Trust, England, and Pohakuloa Game Farm, Hawaii, and Litchfield, Connecticut, USA. Birds successfully reintroduced to wild.	Continued captive breeding programs, more reserves in wild, control of wild predators, improvement of habitat.	☆☆☆☆☆★★
Persecution by man, and extensive deforestation of its favored wooded wetlands and virgin forests. Little is known about it, making it difficult to protect.	Complete protection. Provision of food during cold winters. Efforts to secure breeding and feeding places.	No additional measures proposed.	☆★★★★

135

Key on page 137

SPECIES		RANGE	POPULATION
SPANISH IMPERIAL EAGLE (*Aquila heliaca adalberti*)	Distinguished from other large eagles by white shoulders. Builds huge conspicuous nest in isolated tall tree. Sluggish behavior.	Central and southern Spain, also northern Morocco and north-eastern Algeria. Formerly may have extended as far north as Pyrenees.	Not known to breed outside Spain, where total population not more than a hundred. Most endangered bird in Europe.
GALÁPAGOS FLIGHTLESS CORMORANT (*Nannopterum harrisi*)	Evolved to flightless state in island isolation. Rudimentary wings not used for flight or swimming, but spreads them out to dry after swimming—perhaps a relic of evolutionary past.	Confined to Albemarle and Narborough Islands, in Galápagos group, Pacific Ocean.	Numbers estimated at 3,000-5,000 in 1962; declined to perhaps 1,000 birds today. Accurate assessment difficult.
TRUMPETER SWAN (*Cygnus buccinator*)	The largest North American swan, 6 feet long. A huge, all-white swimming bird, similar to the whistling swan, but with a louder, lower-pitched, more bugle-like call.	Alaska, British Columbia, Alberta, Idaho, Montana, Wyoming. Formerly widespread through western and southern United States, and other parts of Canada.	At one time reduced to about sixty in US excluding Alaska, but numbers increased to more than 2,000, of which several hundred probably in Alaska.
GREEN TURTLE (*Chelonia mydas*)	A marine reptile, found in the warm seas. Spends almost its whole life in the water apart from the period of egg-laying. Can weigh up to 1,000 lbs, but usually much smaller. About 500 soft-shelled eggs laid by female every third year, on tropical beaches above high-tide mark. Perhaps the most valuable reptile in the world.	Eastern Caribbean, South Atlantic, Indian, and Pacific Oceans.	Impossible to estimate current numbers, but severe drop in past twenty years.
DEVIL'S HOLE PUPFISH (*Cyprinodon diabolis*)	One-inch long relict of Pliocene period. One of several cyprinodon fishes which evolved separately in very restricted habitats in desert of American south-west.	Isolated for 30,000-50,000 years in Devil's Hole, a single spring-fed pool fifty feet down in Ash Meadows, Nevada, near Death Valley, California—the lowest, hottest, driest place in the US. In this spring, the fish are confined to area of water twelve inches deep above a single ledge.	In summer when direct sunlight stimulates algae growth, pupfish numbers rise to 700; in winter, algae and small invertebrates dwindle, so pupfish numbers drop to 200.

THE PROBLEM	ACTION TAKEN	ACTION NEEDED	SURVIVAL RATING / POPULATION TREND
Victim of continuous persecution by man—who is everywhere suspicious of birds of prey. Nesting areas becoming scarcer as human population grows and spreads.	Probably none, except protection of large area of natural habitat in Coto Doñana, Spain's great National Park. Seven pairs have nested there in the cork oaks.	Full legal protection needed; without it, unlikely to survive.	☆☆★★★★
Hunting for meat and eggs; collecting for zoos; and more recently, killed in lobster pots set in area (cormorants feed along sea floor). Possible disturbance from increased tourism.	Protected by law (Government of Ecuador), but little enforcement possible as habitat virtually uninhabited by man.	Further studies of species in the wild. Investigate ways to conserve birds and habitat.	☆☆☆★★★
The species gradually receded in face of the advance of civilization. Hunting a major cause of decline.	Hunting prohibited in US and Canada. Undoubtedly saved in US by creation of Red Rock Lake Refuge in the Yellowstone in 1935. Successful captive breeding in Nevada, S. Dakota.	Translocation of young birds to widen further the bird's range.	☆☆☆☆☆★★
Calipee (the cartilaginous material in the bellyshell) in demand for soup; oil for cosmetics; leather for shoes and purses. Eggs taken in thousands from nesting beaches. Natural predation on young hatchlings.	Protective measures in some nesting and feeding areas. Transplanting eggs to special hatcheries for subsequent release in sea. In Queensland, Australia, protected along 3,200 miles of beaches and 1,200 miles of Barrier Reef.	Investigate other hatching, rearing sites. Develop captive breeding to take strain off wild populations. Full protection for present nesting beaches. Hotels, roads, people to be kept as far away as possible from nesting beaches.	☆☆☆☆★★★★★
Water extraction nearby caused water level in spring to drop dangerously. Although pumping has stopped, water has not risen and pupfish now nearly deprived of habitat above ledge.	Water pumping stopped by Department of Justice order. Unsuccessful attempts at transplanting to alternative habitats. Captive breeding attempts also unsuccessful.	Further attempts at transplanting and captive breeding. But scientific importance lies in maintaining population in Devil's Hole. Establishment of a refuge embracing this and nearby Ash Meadows springs (home of endangered relative, the Nevada pupfish) considered vital by Desert Fishes Council.	☆☆☆★★★

KEY TO SURVIVAL RATING		KEY TO POPULATION TREND	
Survival in the wild seems assured	☆☆☆☆☆	*Wild population* increasing rapidly	★
,, likely	☆☆☆☆	,, increasing moderately	★★
,, possible	☆☆☆	,, steady	★★★
,, unlikely	☆☆	,, decreasing moderately	★★★★
,, very unlikely	☆	,, decreasing rapidly	★★★★★

World Wildlife Fund

The World Wildlife Fund was born just over ten years ago when it became obvious that something urgent had to be done to halt the growing threat of extinction facing large numbers of animals and plants—and also the increasing rate of destruction of wilderness areas. The Fund's task is primarily to raise money to finance conservation action. Working in close conjunction with its sister organization, the International Union for Conservation of Nature and Natural Resources, which provides it with scientific guidance, World Wildlife finances projects on a world scale. Many of the people who donate money to World Wildlife may never see the animals or places they are helping to save. But they share a common desire that they should be saved for future generations to enjoy.

Though much of World Wildlife's support goes to conserve species threatened with extinction, it is more and more tending to preserve wilderness areas. For in the long run, all attempts to save individual species are doomed to failure unless their habitat is secure. Key areas include wetlands, tropical rainforests, oceanic islands, coastal and estuarine zones, circumpolar regions, desert and semi-desert areas, and high mountains.

Recently described by *Time* magazine as having grown from 'an obscure club of wealthy do-gooders to the UN of conservation', World Wildlife now has branches (known as National Appeals) in eighteen countries, with more in the process of formation. It has supported some 700 different projects in over sixty countries to the tune of over $9 million (about £3.5 million).

The philosophy behind this great international effort is well summed up in the words of three famous Americans. 'Conservation can be defined as the wise use of our natural environment,' said President John F. Kennedy, 'It is, in the final analysis, the highest form of national thrift.' An earlier President, Theodore Roosevelt, said that 'when I hear of the destruction of a species I feel as if all the works of a great writer had perished.' And General Charles Lindbergh, an International Trustee of the World Wildlife Fund, has written: 'I do not think there is anything more important than conservation, with the exception of human survival, and the two are so closely interlaced that it is hard to separate one from the other.'

HEADQUARTERS
The World Wildlife Fund
1110 Morges, **Switzerland**

President: HRH The Prince of the Netherlands, GCB, GCVO, GBE
Executive Vice-President: Dr Luc Hoffmann
Vice-President and Chairman: Peter Scott, CBE, DSC, LLD
Hon. Treasurer: Graham D. Mattison
Director-General: Dr Fritz Vollmar

Austria
Österreichischer Stifterverband für Naturschutz, angeschlossen dem World Wildlife Fund
Colloredogasse 24
1180 Vienna

Belgium
The World Wildlife Fund (Belgium)
Rue Vautier, 31
B – 1040 Bruxelles 4

Canada
World Wildlife Fund (Canada)
60 St. Clair Av. East
Suite 201
Toronto 7, Ontario

Denmark
Verdensnaturfonden (WWF Denmark)
Kavalergarden 1
2920 Charlottenlund
Copenhagen

Finland
Maailman Luonnon Säätiö
Suomen Rahasto
Korkeavuorenkatu 30A
00131 Helsinki 13

Germany
Verein zur Förderung des World Wildlife Fund e.V.
Postfach 120 363
53 Bonn

India
World Wildlife Fund (India)
c/o Bombay Natural History Society
Hornbill House
Prince of Wales Museum Compound
Bombay 1

Italy
Associazione Italiana per il World Wildlife Fund
Via P.A. Micheli 62
Rome

Norway
World Wildlife Fund (Norway)
Prinsens Gate 22
Oslo

Netherlands
Wereld Natuur Fonds (Nederland)
Stichting Het, P.O. Box 7
Zeit

Malaysia
World Wildlife Fund (Malaysia)
8th Floor, Wisma Damansara
Jalan Semantan
P.O. Box 769
Kuala Lumpur

Pakistan
The Pakistan Wildlife Appeal
c/o Packages Ltd
Rumi Road
Lahore 14

South Africa
The S.A. Nature Foundation
Die S.A. Natuurstigting
P.O. Box 456
Stellenbosch

Spain
ADENA
José Lazaro Galdiano 4
Madrid – 16

Sweden
World Wildlife Fund (Sweden)
Fituna
S–140 41 Sorunda

Switzerland
World Wildlife Fund (Switzerland)
Rieterstrasse 6
Postfach 8027 Zurich

United Kingdom
The World Wildlife Fund, British National Appeal
7 Plumtree Court
London EC4

United States
The World Wildlife Fund Inc
Suite 619
910 Seventeenth Street, N.W.
Washington, DC 20006

Credits

Cover–Stan Wayman/Life Magazine; **2-3**–Mark Boulton/Bruce Coleman; **6**–Eric Hosking; **8**–Russ Kinne/Bruce Coleman; **10**–The White House, Washington; Guy Coheleach; **11**–BBC; David Shepherd; **12-13**–Stan Wayman/Life Magazine; **14**–Alexander Low; **15**–Adolf Schmidecker; **16**–Stan Wayman/Life Magazine; L. R. Coudoux; Tony Beamish; **17**–Anne Wright; **18-19**–John Dominis/Life Magazine; **20-21**–Norman Myers/Bruce Coleman; George Schaller/Bruce Coleman; Dick Robinson/Bruce Coleman; **22**–Fritz Vollmar/WWF; **23**–Abril Press; Brenard Photographic Press; Norman Myers/Bruce Coleman; **24**–Hermann Rijksen; **27**–Tony Carding; **28**–Sven Gillsäter; **30-31**–Joe Rychetnik/Transworld Feature Syndicate; **32**–Novosti Press; **33**–Sven Gillsäter; **35**–Stan Wayman/Life Magazine; **36**–Zoological Society of London; **38**–Alain Schilling/Bruce Coleman; **41**–Helmut Diller/WWF; **43-45**–Robert Martin; **47-48**–Nigel Sitwell; **49**–Hilmi Oesman; **51**–Roger Tory Peterson/Bruce Coleman; **53**–Hans D. Dossenbach; **54**–Mansell Collection; **55**–Sven Gillsäter; **56-58**–Christopher Mylne; **59**–R. Fyfe; **61**–Shelly Grossman/Woodfin Camp; **63**–Cameron Kepler; **68-69**–Terence Spencer; **70**–Nigel Sitwell; Peter Johnson; **72**–Terence Spencer; **72-73**–Peter Johnson; **73**–Malcolm Penny; **74**–F. Pedrotti; **74-75**–De Biasi; **75**–F. Pedrotti; **76-77**–Gordon Williamson; **78**–Des & Jen Bartlett/Bruce Coleman; **80**–Adam Woolfit; **81**–Gordon Williamson; Adam Woolfit; **82**–J. & S. Brownlie/Bruce Coleman; Dorothy Gourley/Bruce Coleman; **83**–Des & Jen Bartlett/Bruce Coleman; **85-87**–Francisco Erize; **88**–Fred Bruemmer; **89**–Syndication International; **91-93**–Karl Kenyon; Tom Myers; **94-95**–David Hughes/Bruce Coleman; **97**–Patricia Caulfield; **99**–Alan Band Associates; **100-102**–A. Hutson; **103**–Peter Johnson/NHPA; **104-6**–Sven Gillsäter/TIO; **107**–Peter Pritchard/WWF; Eric Hosking; **108-109**–F. Baillie; **110**–Jane Burton/Bruce Coleman; **111**–Vic Savage; **112-114**–Tom Myers; **115**–Norman Myers/Bruce Coleman; **117**–R. Melville; **118**–P. Green; N. R. Kerr; R. Melville; **119**–P. Green; R. Melville; **122-125**–WeHa Photo; **126**–Georg Gerster/John Hillelson; **127**–Ernst Haas/John Hillelson; Fritz Vollmar/WWF; **128**–Leonard Lee Rue IV/Bruce Coleman; Joe Van Wormer/Bruce Coleman; James Tallon/NHPA; **129**–Social Security Adm/National Archives.

Poachers Still Hunt the Alligator reprinted on **pages 94-99** by permission of *Audubon* magazine; tabular information on **page 37** from *Men and Pandas* by Desmond Morris and drawings of whales on **page 79** from *The Lost Leviathan* by F. D. Ommanney reprinted by permission of Hutchinson Publishing Group Ltd; chart on **page 26** from the *International Zoo Yearbook;* drawings on **pages 132-137** by Denys Ovenden by permission of Collins and the Wildlife Youth Service; parrots on **pages 64-65** from *Birds of the West Indies* reprinted by permission of Collins.

Index

Acinonyx jubatus **132**
Africa **20**
Ailanthus altissima **118**
Ailanthus fordii **118**
Aldabra **101**
Aleutians **92**
Alkaloids **119**
Alligator hides **95-99**
Alligator mississippiensis **98**
Alligators **19, 95-99**
Amblonyx cinerea **90**
Amchitka Island **92**
Amphibians **94**
Antarctic **84, 87**
Aonyx capensis **90**
Aquila heliaca adalberti **136**
Arctic **28**
Arctocephalus **88**
Argentina **52, 54**
Aride **73**
Ashoka **50**
Atropine **119**
Audubon's or dusky shearwater **73**

Balaenoptera physalus **134**
Bali tiger **13**
Barber, Janet **34**
Bare-legged scops owl **71**
Barn owl **71**
Bawean deer **46-49**
Beamish, Tony **101**
Bengal tiger **14**
Bijleveld, I. J. **126**
Bijleveld, M. F. **126**
Bikaner, Maharajah of **14**
Bilharzia **119**
Bird-netting **74**
Bird-watchers **9**
Birds **8, 56**
   of Carmargue **125**
   of Italy **74-75**
   of Nakuru **126**
   of Seychelles **68-73**
Bison, European **132**
Bison bonasus **132**
Black paradise fly-catcher **70, 71**
Black parrot **71**
Blue pigeon **71**
Blushing bride **118**
Bolivar, Simon **50**
Bolivia **50, 55**
Borneo **24**
Boswall, Jeffery **52**
Botswana **22**
Branta sandvicensis **134**
Brazil **19**

Bridled terns **73**
British Isles **58**
British Trust for Ornithology **58**
Brooklyn tree **118**
Brush warbler **68, 71**
Bryde's whale **79**
Bulbul **71**
Burton, John **108**
Butterflies **9, 108-11**

Calabrian primrose **118**
Camargue **122-25**
Canada **60, 87**
Canadian Wildlife Service **60**
Caras, Roger A. **10**
Carson, Rachel **8**
Caspian tiger **14**
Castro, Miguel **104**
Catharanthus roseus **119**
Cervus duvauceli **134**
Charles Darwin Foundation **104**
Chatham Island **104**
Cheetah **18-23, 132**
Chelonia mydas **136**
Chile **50**
China **34**
Chinese tiger **14**
Chlorinated hydrocarbons **9**
Christoph, Shawn **30**
Coheleach, Guy **10**
Coipasa **50**
Colombia **19**
Committee on Seals and
   Sealing (COSS) **87**
Coquerel's mouse **43**
Cormorant, Galápagos flightless **136**
Cousin Island **68-72**
Crane, whooping **134**
Cutillo, D. J. **52**
Cygnus buccinator **136**
Cyprinodon diabolis **136**
Cypripedium calcelus **116**

Darwin, Charles **40, 103**
David, Père Armand **34**
Davies, Jack **87**
DDE **59**
DDT **8, 59, 60**
Deer, swamp **134**
   see also Bawean deer
de Silva, G. S. **26**
Devil's hole pupfish **136**
Dieldrin **59**
Digitalin **118**
Digoxin **118**

Dolphins **82**
Dominica **67**
Dominican Republic **67**
Drugs **118, 119**
Duncan Island **104, 105**
Duplaix-Hall, Nicole **90**

Eagle **9**
   Spanish imperial **136**
Edinburgh, HRH The Duke of **7**
Emergency action summary **130-31**
Endangered Species Conservation
   Act **96, 98**
Enhydra lutris **90**
Erica jasminiflora **118**
Erica junonia **118**
Erosion **127**
European bison **132**
European Conservation Year **74**
Everglades Park **19**

Fairy tern **71**
Falkland Islands **87**
Félicite **70**
Fertilizers **127**
Fisher, James **9**
Flamingoes **126**
Fodies **71**
Ford's tree of heaven **118**
Foxglove **118**
France **122**
Frankfurt Zoological Society **54**
Frazier, Jack **102**
Frazier, Willard J. **96**
Frigate Island **70**
Fur, sea otter **90-93**
Fur trade **18-23**
Fyfe, Richard **59**

Galápagos flightless cormorant **136**
Galápagos Islands **40, 101, 103**
Giant pandas **34-37, 42**
   in captivity outside China and
   Korea **37**
Golden lion marmoset **134**
Goodwin, Robin **11**
Goose, Hawaiian **134**
Grant, Ulysses S. **128**
Gray white-eye **71**
Greater frigate **73**
Greenland **32, 84**
Green turtle **136**
Grus americana **134**
Guadeloupe **67**

Gulf of St Lawrence **84**
Gunung Loeser Reserve **24**

Habitats, destruction **108**
   saving **120**
Harkness, Ruth **37**
Harrisson, Barbara **25**
Harrisson, Tom **24**
Hawaiian goose **134**
Heathers **118**
Heptachlor epoxide **59**
Hispaniolan parrot **63**
Hofmann, R. **55**
Hood **104**
Hydrurga leptonyx **88**
Hyelaphus kuhlii **46**
Hyoscine **119**

Ibis, Japanese crested **134**
Idea leuconoe **111**
Inca Empire **50**
Incas **54**
Indefatigable Island **105**
Indian Ocean **101**
Indian tiger **14**
Indo-Chinese tiger **14**
Indonesia **13, 46**
Insects **108**
International Council for Bird
   Preservation **68, 71**
International Union for the
   Conservation of Nature **19, 25, 32,**
   45, 52, 54, 116, 130, 131
International Whaling Commission
   78, 81, 88
Italy **74-75**
Ixias pyrene **110**

Jade vine pea **116**
Jaguar **19, 21, 23**
Jan Mayen Island **84**
Japan **19, 81, 82, 83, 88**
Japanese crested ibis **134**
Jasmine heather **118**
Javan rhinoceros **132**
Javan tiger **13**
Johnson, Lyndon **115**
Jungius, Hartmut **50**
Juno heath **118**

Kennedy, John F. **138**
Kensinger, William R. **96**
Kenya **19, 20, 126**

Kepler, Cameron **62**
Kestrel **71**
King, F. Wayne **98**
Kong Karl's Land **28, 32**
Kurile Islands **92**

Labrador **84**
La Digue **70**
Lake Nakuru **126**
Latin America **19**
Laycock, George **95**
Lemur macaco sandfordi **43**
Lemurs **37-45**
   aye-aye **41, 44**
   brown **41, 43**
   brown dwarf **43**
   current status **42**
   fat-tailed dwarf **43**
   fork-crowned **41, 43**
   mouse **43**
   ring-tailed **43, 45**
   small-bodied dwarf **43**
   sportive **44**
   vertical-clinging-and-leaping **44**
Leontideus rosalia **134**
Leopard **19-21**
   snow **21**
Leptonychotes weddelli **88**
Leticia **19**
Lima **52**
Lindane **59**
Lindbergh, Charles **138**
Little terns **73**
Lobodon carcinophagus **88**

McHugh, J. L. **78**
MacKinnon, John **26**
Madagascar **40**
Magpie robin **70**
Mahé **70, 71**
Malaysia **17**
Mammals, large **12**
   smaller **38**
Marianne **70**
Marine environment **76**
Marine pollution **59**
Marmoset, golden lion **134**
Martin, Robert **37**
Martinique **67**
Melville, Ronald **116**
Mercury **60**
Milne-Edwards, Alphonse **34**
Mirounga leonina **88**
Morne Diablotin **67**
Moths **9**

Mountfort, Guy **13**
Mouse lemur **43**
Muir, John **112**
Muller, Salomon **46**
Mutton bird **73**
Myers, Norman **18**

Nakuru, Lake **126**
Nannopterum harrisi **136**
Nature Conservancy **58**
Nipponia nippon **134**
Noddies **73**
North America **59**
Norway **32, 87**
Nossi Mangabé **45**

Ocelot **19**
Ommatophoca rossi **88**
Operation Tiger **17**
Orang-utan **24-27**
Orchids **118**
Organochlorine pesticides **58**
Organochlorine seed treatments **60**
Ornithoptera **108**
Ornithoptera allottei **111**
Ornithoptera victoria **111**
Ornithopterans **108**
Osio, Arturo **74**
Osprey **9**
OURS (Orang-Utan Recovery
   Service) **25**

Pagophilus groenlandicus **84**
Pampas Galeras **52**
Panthera tigris tigris **132**
Papilios **108**
Parakeets **62**
Parrots **62-67**
   amazon **66**
   black-billed **67**
   Cuban **66**
   Hispaniolan **63, 67**
   imperial **67**
   Puerto Rican **62**
   red-necked **67**
   West Indian **62**
   past and present distribution and
     status **66**
   yellow-billed **66**
Pelican **9**
Penny, Malcolm **68**
Peregrine falcon **9, 56-61**
   in Britain **58**
   in N. America **59**

Peregrine Symposium 59
Perry, Roger 103
Peru 19, 50, 54, 55
Pesticides 8, 58, 59, 127
Peterson, Roger Tory 8, 126
Petter, Jean-Jacques 44
Philip, Prince, HRH The Duke of
    Edinburgh 7
Phillip Island glory pea 116
Phytolacca dodecandra 119
Pie 70
Plants 108, 112, 116-19
Platt, Colin 84
Plott, Christopher Joel 96
Plott, Quince Clayton 96
Polar bears 28-33, 132
Pollution 9, 92
    marine 59
Polychlorinated biphenyls (PCBs) 59
Pongo pygmaeus   *See* Orang-utan
Porpoises 82
Praslin 70
Primula palinuri 118
Puerto Rico 62

Raptor Research Foundation 60
Ratcliffe, Derek 58
Rauvolfia serpentina 119
Reagan, Ronald 115
Red Data Book 44, 67, 68, 116, 119, 130
Red-tailed tropicbird 73
Redwood 112-15, 118
Redwood National Park 112
Reptiles 94
Rhinoceros, Javan 132
Rhinoceros sondaicus 132
Roosevelt, Kermit 37
Roosevelt, Theodore 37, 138
Roseate terms 73
Rosy periwinkle 119
Rotmann, J. 52
Russia 32, 81, 83

Sage, Dean, Jr. 37
St Helena 118
St Lucia 67
St Vincent 67
Sanders, Robert 128
Sandford's lemur 43
San Guillermo 54
Savage, Christopher 122
Scotland 58
Scott, Peter 37, 116, 119
Sea otter 90-93
Sealing 84-88

Seals 84-88
    elephant 87
    harp 84
        growth cycle 88
Sekers Fabrics Ltd. 110
Sepilok Reserve 27
Serruria florida 118
Seychelles, birds of 68-73
Shepherd, David 11
Siberian tiger 14
Sifaka 45
Silent Spring 8
Sitwell, Nigel 11, 46, 77
Skins, spotted cat 19
    tiger 17
Smith, Floyd Tangier 37
Smyth, John V. 112
Snowy egrets 10
Soapberry 119
Solomon Islands 111
Sooty terns 73
Soviet Union. *See* Russia
Spanish imperial eagle 136
Spitzbergen 32
Spotted cat skins 19
Spotted cats 18-23
Steele, Harold 98
Stonegate, David 28
Strebblorhiza speciosa 116
Streptopelia picturata 71
Strong, Maurice 78
Strongylodon macrobotrys 116
Sudan 19
Sumatra 14, 24
Sunbird 71
Sunda Shelf 46
Surabaja Zoo 49
Svalbard (Spitzbergen) Treaty 32
Swamp deer 134
Swan, trumpeter 136
Szechwan 34

Taman Negara National Park 17
Tananarive 45
Tanzania 20, 23
Terminalia catappa 70
Terns 73
Thalarctos maritimus 132
Tiger skins 16, 17
Tigers 13-17, 20
    current status 17
    Indian 132
Tinker, Jon 116
Tortoises 100
    on Aldabra 101-3

on Galápagos 103
Toxic chemicals 58, 59, 60
Tree of heaven 118
Trees 112, 118
Trochetia erythroxylon 118
Trumpeter swan 136
Tsavo Waterhole 11
Turtle, green 136
Turtle dove 71

Uganda 20
UNESCO 127
United States 32, 83, 95-99, 112, 128
US Bureau of Sport Fisheries and
    Wildlife 32
US Forest Service 62
Uyuni 50

Van Bemmel 46
Venezuela 19
Vicuna 50-55

Wedge-tailed shearwater 72
West Indian parrot 62, 66
Wetlands 122
Wetmore, Alexander 62
Whales 77-83
    blue 78
    Bryde's 79
    fin 79, 81, 134
    hump-back 78
    right 78
    sei 79, 81
    sperm 79, 81
Whaling 77-83
    moratorium on 78, 80
    White-tailed tropic-birds 73
Whooping crane 134
Wildlife Crisis 9
Williams, Frederick A. 96
World Wildlife Fund 17, 23, 37, 45, 52,
    54, 55, 58, 74, 116, 125, 127, 131, 138

Yellowstone National Park 128-29